WESTERN EDUCATIONAL THINKERS

About the Authors

Professor S. P. Chaube was born on Feb. 1, 1919 in the district of Varanasi (U. P.). He received his M. A. from Banaras and M. Ed. from Allahabad. Prof. Chaube has travelled extensively throughout U. S. A., U. K. and various European conturies and has closely studied the educational systems of the same.

For doing research for a doctorate degree, Dr. Chaube was appointed in 1950 a fellow by the University of Indiana, Bloomington, U. S. A. which conferred on him the degree of Doctor of Education in 1952 on a thesis pertaining to the area of philosophical foundations of Secondary Education in India.

As a mark of his contributions in education in India, Dr. Chaube was decorated with the G. J. Watumull Memorial Award in Education in 1963 by a board of international judges.

Lucknow University conferred on him its D.Litt. degree in 1965. He was also awarded by this University the Banerji Research Prize in 1965 for producing the best research work of the year.

After teaching at the University of Lucknow, Dr. Chaube joined Gorakhpur University from where he retired as a Professor of Education & Dean, Faculty of Education in 1979.

Dr. Chaube's works, particularly, in the fields of "Education" and "Psychology" are taught in universities through out India. He has more than 50 books to his credit both in Hindi and English under these two discipline, out of these 50, more than a dozen books in English pertain to the discipline of "Psychology".

Dr. Akhilesh Chaube, b. 1952, M. Sc. (Botany), M. Ed., M. Phil. & Ph.D., University teaching experience of two decades. Currently, Reader in Education at the University of Lucknow.

Western Educational Thinkers

PROF. S. P. CHAUBE
M.A., M.Ed. (Alld.)
D.Ed. (Indiana, U.S.A.), D. Litt. (Lucknow)
Recipient of the G. J. Watumull
Memorial Award in Education,
Retired : Dean & Professor of Education,
University, Gorakhpur (U.P.)

DR. AKHILESH CHAUBE
M.Sc., M.Ed., M.Phil., Ph.D.
Reader, Education Department,
Institute of Advanced Studies in Education,
Lucknow University, Lucknow

CONCEPT PUBLISHING COMPANY, NEW DELHI - 110059

ISBN-81-7022-935-9 (PB)

First Published 2002

Published and Printed by
Ashok Kumar Mittal
Concept Publishing Company
A/15-16, Commercial Block, Mohan Garden,
NEW DELHI-110 059

Phones : 5648039, 5649024
Fax : 091-11-5648053
Email : publishing@concept.com

Preface

Western educational thinkers are compulsorily taught to students of Education of B.A., B.Ed. and M.Ed. classes as a part of the course in philosophy of education or as educational philosophers. This book is principally designed to meet the curricular demands of such graduate and post-graduate classes. Herein an attempt has been made to present the subject matter in a compact but in all — inclusive and lucid manner. Any way, it is the readers to judge the extent to which the authors have succeeded in their objectives. Neverthless, if this venture on their part propels one to make an advanced study of any educational thinkers herein included for discussion, the authors will feel amply rewarded.

S.P. CHAUBE
AKHILESH CHAUBE

Karma Bhumi,
B-955, Sector -A,
Near New Railway Crossing,
Mahanagar
Lucknow-226006

CONTENTS

1

PLATO

(427 or 429 B.C. — 47 B.C.)

His Life

Plato, the first western educational philosopher, was born in Athens in 427 or 429 B.C. Plato represented the highest Athenian talent of the day. Very little is known about his early education. At the age of twenty or so he became closely attached to Socrates as his disciple and remained with him for ten years. At this time Socrates was over sixty years of age.

Plato has given to the world a general philosophy embracing a theory of a new form of government, and a new social order. He has also pleaded for an educational system on which these two are to be based. He has propounded the first comprehensive system of philosophy which has become the forerunner of all the later idealistic theories. He has viewed the world with an open mind, so his philosophy has always been of abiding interest. He has influenced political science, religion and education throughout the succeeding ages. Though he is abstract and transcendental, it is difficult for a student of education to ignore his theories. First of all we shall try to understand his idealism.

THE PLATONIC IDEALISM

The Nature of Plato's Philosophy

teachableness of virtue Plato realised that first of all he should understand the nature of man and of the world; and the inter-relation between the two. For this, he has propounded theories which are highly abstract and difficult to understand. He did not choose to give us an elaborate philosophy. He has just projected some transcendent ideas and ideals and expects that the individual should form his own conclusion. Thus, he has not advocated any dogmatic and final system.

Plato's Theory of Knowledge

Innateness of Knowledge

Plato holds that true knowledge is innate. He thinks that knowledge does not come to the soul at or after birth. In fact, it is a part of the soul itself, and it is always with the soul. This conception has led Plato to conclude that soul existed before the body and during the prenatal existence it learned all that with which it is familiar in this world.

The Three Kinds of Knowledge

Plato has spoken of three kinds of knowledge : (1) The first kind of knowledge is that which comes through senses, such as sour, cold, smooth and colour. To Plato the knowledge that is derived through senses is not true, because senses are not real. (2) The second kind of knowledge is that of opinion regarding things. An opinion about things may be valuable in certain situations, but it cannot be true knowledge, nor is it innate. (3) The third kind of knowledge, which alone is true is innate and is in the mind or reason. All mathematical truths, general concepts, absolute and abstract ideas fall within this category. Absolute ideas about beauty, justice, goodness are never acquired through experience. They are innate and the possession of the mind itself, independent of experience.

If true knowledge is innate, why does an infant not exhibit its presence at birth; and how is such knowledge recalled? Plato has not answered this question satisfactorily, and has taken recourse to a myth for explaining it. He says that soul had the knowledge of reality in a former existence. At birth when the soul joins a body, it forgets its true knowledge. Later, the true knowledge is brought back to the mind by process of reminiscence. But how did this innate knowledge come to the soul in the former state of being ? Plato is not clear at this point. However, we shall see below under the section 'Plato's Psychology' how Plato answers this question.

To Plato there are two kinds of worlds — the world of ideas and the world of objects of senses. The world of ideas is real and the other is only a shadow of phenomenal. The world of ideas is eternal, spaceless and unchangeable. It is the world of mind, a world of abstract thought. It is true and genuine and apart from the things of earth. The absolute ideas are entities in themselves, and they form an organic whole, a 'World of Ideas'. To Plato ideas are interrelated in a divine order or perfect mind. The 'World of Ideas' is the mind of God. Ideas are eternal divine thoughts. They are God's. It is after their pattern that the things of earth are modelled because they are perfect in themselves; in other words, they are ideal and perfect things. Such is the nature of Platonic idealism. It regards that true reality is thought, and therefore, it is spiritual. Thus, to Plato thought alone is true and perfect, and it is apart from material things.

Against the ideal world, there is a material world, the world of senses which has nothing perfect and abiding in it. In the world of senses everything is in space and time, everything is subject to change — nothing is permanent. The world of senses is not permanent, because it is made of matter, and it is only a copy or shadow of the real. Plato regards matter as the source of all evils, the cause of all imperfections.

Plato's Psychology

Plato makes a clear cut distinction between soul and body, the subjective and objective. He regards man as the epitome of the universe having two elements — the soul, and the body. The soul has three distinct parts :

(1) The lowest part consisting of desires and appetites, which we call instincts or drives to-day;
(2) The second part is that of courage or spirit which rises from the heart. It is the source of all such alimentary virtues as endurance, hardihood and perseverance. These two parts of the soul belong to the body. Hence, they decay and die with the body; and
(3) The highest part of the soul is reason. Its connection is with another world. It is not earthly. It is divine and has no affinity with the body. The body works as a prison house to the soul of reason.

However, reason survives the destruction of the body. Reason resides in the head, the most dignified part of the body. Thus, Plato regarded brain as the seat of the mind—the reason.

Plato's Theory of Ethics

Plato believed that "Good" was the highest reality in the universe hence everything must contribute to it. He thought that for being moral one must possess certain virtues or "Goods of the Soul", as he has called them. The virtues or "Goods" a red justice self-control, magnanimity and temperance. These virtues have their root in the psychological nature of man. Each element of the soul has its corresponding virtue. For the appetites, self-control is the important virtue. Courage is the virtue of the heart. To Plato self-control and coverage are the fundamental virtues for individual and civil life. Justice is the final virtue. Justice helps man to maintain an inter-relationship between the various elements of his complex nature. The capacity for justice helps other faculties of the soul to carry on their proper function. Appetites should be curbed. Courage should be the active wisdom and reason should decide things all times. These are the demands of justice.

The Source of Evil

Plato regarded the material world as against the World of Ideas or of the Good. The material world is the source of all evils. It is subject to decay and death. The human body shares all the weaknesses and deprivations of the material world. That is why the appetites was against the mind. The body deprives the reason and it is worse than a prison to the soul. Thus, Plato regarded body as the source of all evil. This view had been greatly misinterpreted by some Christian thinkers and have led education to adopt a hostile attitude to the human physique.

Theory of Government

Plato has given us his philosophy of government through the Republic and the Laws. He accepted the traditional belief that the individuals should be trained as tools of the state in order to defend it and administer its affairs. He regarded the state as an organism or personality, just like an individual, having all the faculties of the individual writ large. Everything that is found in the individual exists in the state in a much greater measure. Corresponding to the three faculties of the soul—the appetites, spirit and reason, the state consists of there classes of people: (1) the vast body of people like the appetites of the soul; (2) the "guardians", or army or police like the soul of courage; or (3) the ruling class—the reason of the state corresponding to the reason of the soul.

Plato did not believe that the best interests of the individual and those of the state would ever be into serious conflict. If the state is functioning in a healthy manner, its parts, i.e., the individuals, too, will be in good health.

Plato considered the state as to divine agency with a divine function. Its divine function is to realize the Good upon the earth after the model of absolute justice. Thus, the state has ethical ends.

Plato on the Family

Plato was not favourably inclined towards family as a good

institution. He did not like 'individualizing tendencies of family life'. To him the welfare of the state was paramount, and there was no value of family associations against the state. During the old Athenian period the family had failed to train children and produce able citizens. This failure had weakened the state. So, Plato considered the state above family associations and recommended state control of the breeding, nursing, and training of children. Plato permitted family life to the slaves only. Thus, Plato appears to be a staunch advocate of the state control of education.

Plato on Women

Plato remained a bachelor all through his life and he failed to understand the distinctive traits of feminine nature. He thought that the females have fundamentally the same nature as males, though they are not so strong. However, he is prepared to admit women to all the offices and work of the state.

PLATO'S PHILOSOPHY OF EDUCATION

Plato placed an exalted value on education. Therefore, in all his works the problem of education finds a place. The Republic and the Laws have education as their major theme. To him education is "the first and fairest thing that the best of men can ever have".[1] During his long life time his ideas underwent an evolution. In the Republic he spoke of "an ideal state and idealistic and intellectualistic view of education". In the Laws, written in old age, he gave up his idealism and showed extreme conservatism.

What is Education

Plato regarded education as a process of moral training. Education is an effort on the part of the older generation to pass on to younger generation all the good habits and wisdom acquired through experience. Plato says, "I mean by education that training which is given by suitable habits to the first instincts of virtue in children. . . . which leads you always to hate what you ought to hate, and love what you ought to love, from the beginning of life to the end.... in my view, will be rightly called Education".[2]

The Functions and Purposes of Education

Plato regarded education as "an essential function of the cosmic order". He recognized two kinds of mind, the empirical and the rational. The empirical mind begins from the parts and proceeds to the whole and the rational mind begins from the whole and moves towards the parts. Plato, an idealist, always placed the end above the means, the whole above the parts.

To Plato, the first function and purpose of education is to ascertain state unity. Under the influence of the Sophists the Greek youths had become extremely individualistic in temperament, and the safety of the state was in danger. Plato stood against this social order and advocated for the absolute supremacy of the state. So, Plato wanted to destroy individualism. For this he regarded education as the chief remedy. To him the first purpose of education is to develop a team and co-operative spirit, a feeling of community life. Every citizen must be trained to forego his private interests for the sake of the state. He must dedicate himself fully to the service of the state. In this view, Plato accepted the Spartan ideal of social solidarity, but he went much ahead the Spartan ideology by making "the state a personality that possessed within itself all the factors of body and mind".

The second purpose of education, according to Plato was, to develop civic efficiency which was a great virtue to him. He thought to develop this virtue by inculcating "the habits of temperance, courage and military skill into the youth".

The third purpose of education is to develop the rule of reason in the youth so that the appetites may not have the upper hand.

The fourth purpose of education is to produce a love of truth, beauty and goodness in the child. At birth the child is a creature of low appetites. So, he must be taught to rise above these in order to love the ideal above the actual.

The fifth task of education is to harmonize the personality of the individual. "Body and mind, the life of habit and the life of reason, the individual interests and the interests of the state" must be harmonized for becoming a unified whole.

Plato[3] says, "If our citizens are well educated, and grow into sensible men, they will easily see their way through all these, as well as other matters which count, such, for example, as marriage, the possession of women and the procreation of children." This implies that education has to produce a self-governing individual. "Education must be a substitute for state regimentation and innumerable laws". This is the sixth purpose of education.

"True[4] education. . . . will have the greatest tendency to civilize and humanize them in their relations to one another, and to those who are under their protection." In other words, it is the purpose of the school to teach children to live in harmony. Plato wanted to make the school the greatest humanizing and socializing agency.

Education a Duty of the State

Plato is of the opinion that education should be a primary duty of the state. Therefore, in the Republic and the Laws he has said that education should be conducted under the control of the state. We have already referred to Plato's destruct of the family as an organization for producing able citizens. Therefore, he wants to put all the children under the control of the state for education in public schools. All the children must be educated alike, and no child should be allowed to have his own will apart from that of the community.[5]

The Educational Process

Plato has spoken of two kinds of education : (1) Education for practical affairs, and (2) education for service to the state. The first kind of education aims at acquiring skills from the artisans and trade classes. Plato regards this education as mean and illiberal. The true and liberal education is that which prepares the youth for service to the state, that is, which teaches him to develop the ideal perfection of citizenship.

(1) *Education in Virtues*

In the education of the citizen Plato recognizes two levels—education for fundamental virtues, and education for developing a rational virtue.

At first the child will be educated to develop moral attitudes and habits : Plato regarded discipline and music as the appropriate means for this purpose. But as Plato grew older he recommended the formation of habits by regimentation. In the Laws[6] he says, "The great principle of all is that no one of either sex should be without a commander..... but in war and peace he should look to and follow his leader."

(2) *Conversion*

Plato believes that the higher virtues are acquired through the functioning of the rational faculty. He wants that the life senses should be converted to the love of idea reality. The soul should be turned from low interests to high interests. Plato says, "The process. . . . is not the turning over an oyster shell but the turning round of a soul passing from a day which is little better than night to the true say of being, that is, the ascent from below, which we affirm to be true philosophy".[7] Plato believed that this conversion was possible by the study of arithmetic. He says, "Arithmetic has a very great and elevating effect, compelling the soul to reason about abstract numbers, and rebelling the introduction of visible or trangible objects into the argument".[8]

(3) *Compulsory Training*

According to Plato, compulsory training is necessary for all boys and girls who want to become citizens. But he did not like compulsion in learning. He regarded coercion as painful. Compulsion with regard to bodily exercise is not harmful, but compulsory learning is harmful to the growth of a healthy mind. Plato says, "A freeman ought not to be a slave in the acquisition of knowledge of any kind. Bodily exercise, when compulsory, does no harm to the body; but knowledge, which is acquired under compulsion, obtains no hold on the mind. Then, do not use compulsion, but let early education be a sort of amusement; You will better be above to find out the natural bent".[9] It is only in case of young children that Plato condemns compulsion, for older children he believes in the principle of formal discipline. The compulsory intellectual training is necessary for those who are to look after the affairs of the state.

(4) *Uniformity Necessary*

Plato believes in uniformity which alone, according to him can produce a co-operative spirit so needed for the welfare of the state. Therefore, he demands absolute regimentation in thought and action. He says, the legislator "has only to reflect and find out what belief will be of the greatest public advantage, and then use all his efforts to make the whole community utter one and the same word in their songs and fables and discourses all their life long".[10] Plato is not prepared to accept any change in the routine of youth. He believes in a fixed and unalterable system of training for inculcating moral habits in the youth. Plato has proposed eight rules for carrying out this training :

(i) The environment of children should be moral and should remain unchanged.

(ii) Morals and manners of the young and of every citizen should be under drastic censorship.

(iii) The ancient poetry having any suggestion of evils and falsehood should be eliminated from any educational scheme. Homer should not be taught because of his lies about gods. Song and music should be according to the prescribed models, "Any musical innovation is full of danger to the whole state, and ought to be prohibited.... when modes of music change, the fundamental laws of the state always change with them".[11]

(iv) Persons practising pantomime should be excluded.

(v) Painting, sculpture, and architecture should be regularly censored in order to eliminate their evil influences.

(vi) The games and plays of children must not be changed.

(vii) Reverence for antiquity must be developed.

(viii) The rituals of religion must not be changed. They should remain fixed.

(5) *Women Education*

We have already seen that the men and women have fundamentally the same nature, except that the women are weaker. "All pursuits of men are the pursuits of women also, but in all of them a woman is inferior to a man." If men and women have the same qualities as regards their duties in the state, it means they should have the same education. Plato says that music, dancing, gymnastics, military exercise, housemanship and fighting should be taught both to men and women.

The Courses of Study

Plato's views on curricula are interesting both from philosophic and historical point of view. He has given an outline of curriculum which has been followed in the western countries for more than fifteen centuries. Plato could see the basic principles of child activities which were widely accepted until the advent of Comenius in the seventeenth century. He accepted the traditional Greek curriculum of gymnastics and music for elementary stage but gave a new interpretation to it. For secondary and higher education he proposed a new course of study.

For the first ten years of life, Plato says that the child should be taught arithmetic, plane and solid geometry, music and astronomy. These subjects are not to be studied for calculation, but for understanding the universal relations underlying them. It is only in this way that the capacity for abstract thought can be developed for the secondary stage. Plato recommends the teaching of poetry, arithmetic (especially theory), formal gymnastics and military training, geometry, manners, music and religion.

Plato divides the higher education into two phases— scientific and philosophic. The scientific period is to extend roughly over the years from twenty to thirty. In this period main attention will be on arithmetic, geometry, music and astronomy. After this period five years should be devoted to the study of dialectic.

Plato has originated the disciplinary conception of education. Plato wants to make the disciplinary use of the above subjects at each stage rather than the liberal use. For example, Plato believes that the study of arithmetic will make the child "brighter, quicker and more retentive". He says, "Above all, arithmetic stirs up him who is by nature sleepy and dull, and makes him quick to learn; retentive, shrewd, and aided by art divine, he makes progress quite beyond his natural powers".[12] It means the value of arithmetic lies in the power it provides, and this power can be transferred in other fields as well.

Administration of Education

Plato wants to keep the general charge of educational affairs in the hands of a superintendent of education to be elected by the magistrates from among the ablest citizens of the state. The superintendent should be of over fifty years of age and he should hold office for five years. He should also be given two assistants — on director of music and another for gymnastics. In addition to these there were to be other assistants and superintendents for organizing contests.

Periods of Instruction

Plato has outlined a number of periods for systematic training and instruction according to the stages of development of life.

Infancy : During infancy which extends from birth to three years, the child is to be properly nourished and is to be saved from pain and pleasure as far as possible.

Nursery : According to Plato this period expanding from three to six years of age is the most important part of education. The education during this period should consist of play, fairy tales, other goose and simple recreations.

The Elementary School : This period should begin at six and go upto thirteen. Boys and girls should be housed in separate state dormitories. Plato believes that during this period the children lack in harmony and control and their movements are un-co-ordinated. During this period music, play, religion, morals and mathematics should be taught to children. Plato thinks that education in these will bring the necessary rhythm, melody and control in the behaviour of children.

The Middle School : This period begins at thirteen. Plato says, "The age of thirteen is the proper time for him to begin the lyre, and he may continue at this or another three years. . . . whether his father or himself like or dislike the study, he is not to be allowed to spend more or less time in learning music than the law allows".[13] Hence, this period from thirteen to sixteen is to be devoted to training in instrumental music which consisted of the play of cithera, religious, hymns, memoraize poetry, arithmetic (especially theory).

Gymnastic Period : This period extends from sixteen to twenty. During this period special attention to formal gymnastic and military training should be given. No stress on intellectual training during this period is desirable.

Higher Training : Plato recommends that at the age of twenty the most promising young men and women should be selected through diagnostic tests for a ten years course in scientific studies. At this period the purpose will be to help young men and women to see the inter-relationship of facts, because during this period of growth there is a need of correlating of all thinking. During this period the systematization of the various sciences will be emphasised— there will be co-ordination of reason and habits and inter-relating of the physical sciences. Plato says, "The sciences which they learned without any order in their early education will now be brought together, and they will be able to see the natural relationship of them to one another and to true being".[14]

Training for Officers : Plato has recommended a course for officers selected to serve the state in high offices. This course is for the period from thirty years of age upto thirty-five. The course consists of philosophy, psychology, sociology, government law and education.

Life of Active Duty : Those selected as high officers will serve the state on active duty from thirty-five to fifty.

Philosophers : Plato has recommended that at fifty, the high officers of the state should be relieved from active duty and they should be encouraged to give their attention to the study of higher philosophy.

Plato's Attitude towards the Practical Arts : Plato was not sympathetic to practical arts. He considers them vulgar and unfit for a gentleman. He regards them suitable only for slaves. Therefore, he has given no place to them in his scheme of education. Plato[15] declares, "If any citizen inclines to any other art than the study of virtue let them punish him with disgrace and infamy".

No Education for Slaves : Plato has declined to recommend any system of training for the slaves; because he wants to exclude them from participation in any affairs of the state. He wants that they should follow the traditional family life. He expects the slave boy to follow his father's occupation, and the girl to take part in the household activities of the women. Thus, Plato wants that the slave boy and girl should learn by imitation, because all theory training is only an affair of forming right habits.

SUMMARY

Plato represented the highest Athenian talent of the day. Disciple of Socrates. Has given a general philosophy of government and social order. Forerunner of all later idealistic theories.

The Platonic Idealism

The Nature of Plato's Philosophy : Plato has projected only some transcendent ideas and ideals and expects the individual to form his own conclusion. No dogmatic and final system.

Plato's Theory of Knowledge

Innateness of Knowledge : True knowledge innate. Knowledge a part of the soul which existed before the body.

The Three Kinds of Knowledge : (1) That which comes through the senses. It is not real. (2) Opinion regarding things. Not true knowledge. (3) The mind or reason — the true knowledge. Plato not clear as to how the innate knowledge came to the soul.

Two kinds of world — of ideas and of objects of census. The world of ideas is real and eternal and the other is phenomenal. Ideas inter-related in a divine other. It is after them that the earthly things are modelled. True reality is thought — it is spiritual.

The world of senses not perfect — subject to change— because made of matter. Matter the source of all evils.

Plato's Psychology : A clear-cut distinction between soul and body. Man the epitome of the universe. The soul has three distinct parts — appetite, courage and reason.

Plato's Theory of Ethics : "Good" the highest reality. Virtues or "Goods of the Soul" necessary for being moral. Self-control and courage — the fundamental virtues. is the final virtue.

The Source of Evil : The material world is the source of all evils. The human body shares all the weakness of the material world.

Theory of Government : The Republic and the Laws. Individuals as tools of the state. The state as a personality—having three classes of people : (1) the vast body of the people, (2) the army or police, and (3) the ruling class. The interests of the individual and those of the state are the same.

The state has a divine agency. It has ethical ends.

Plato on the Family : The family not a good institution. The state paramount and above family associations. State control of children. Plato an advocate of state control of education.

Plato on Women : Failed to understand women. To him women and men have the same fundamental nature, though women in a lesser degree. Women to be admitted to all the offices of the state.

Plato's Philosophy of Education

Placed exalted value on education. The Republic and the Laws have education as their major theme.

What is Education : A process of moral training. Transmitting race experience to the younger generation.

The Function and Purposes of Education : Education an essential function of the cosmic order. Two kinds of mind-empirical and rational. The end above the means, the whole above the parts.

(1) To ascertain state unity — education as the chief remedy. The individual to dedicate himself to the service of the state.
(2) To develop civic efficiency.
(3) To develop the rule of reason.
(4) To produce a love of truth, beauty and goodness.
(5) To harmonize the personality of the individual.
(6) To produce a self-governing individual.
(7) To teach children to live a harmony.

Education a Duty of the State : Education a primary duty of the state. All children to be educated in state-controlled public schools.

The Educational Process : Two kinds of education : (1) for practical affairs, and (2) for service to the state the first kind is mean and the second is liberal.

(1) *Education of Virtues* : Education for fundamental virtues and education for a rational virtue. To develop moral attitudes and habits by discipline and music.

(2) *Conversion* : Life of sense to be converted to the love of ideal reality. This conversion possible by the study of arithmetic.

(3) *Compulsory Training* : For all boys and girls. No compulsion in learning. For older children principle of formal discipline.

(4) *Uniformity Necessary* : Absolute regimentation in thought and action necessary. No change in the routine the youth. Eight rules for carrying out this training.

(5) *Women Education* : Both men and women should have the same education.

The Courses of Study : Plato's views important both from philosophical and historical point of view.

For the first ten years arithmetic, plane and solid geometry, music and astronomy in order to understand the universal relations underlying them. For the secondary stage—arithmetic, formal gymnastics, military training, geometry, manners, music and religion. Higher education scientific and philosophic.

Plato originated the disciplinary conception of education.

Administration of Education : A superintendent of education—with two assistants for music and gymnastics.

Periods of Instruction : Infancy, upto three, nourishment. Nursery, upto six, play and tales, etc. The elementary school upto thirteen—for harmonizing and co-ordinating activities of children. The middle school, upto sixteen, training in instrumental music, gymnastic period, upto twenty, formal gymnastics and military training. Higher training, scientific studies upto-thirty. Correlating of all thinking. Training for officers, till thirty five. Life of active duty from thirty five to fifty. Philosophers, after fifty officers of the state to be relieved for the study of higher philosophy.

Plato not sympathetic to practical arts. These are meant for slaves alone.

No education for slaves. They to learn by imitation.

References

1. Laws : 644.
2. Laws : 653.
3. Republic : 423.
4. *Ibid* : 416.
5. Republic : 519-520.
6. Laws : 942.
7. Republic : 521.
8. *Ibid* : 525.
9. *Ibid* : 537.
10. Republic : 664.
11. *Ibid* : 424.
12. Laws : 747.
13. Laws : 810.
14. Republic : 537.
15. Laws : 847.

2

QUINTILLIAN

(35 AD — 100 AD)

Quintillian's Life

No record of Quintillian's birth is found. However, it has been presumed that he was born in the year 35 A.D. or so. His birth place has been Calagurris in Spain. He became greatly interested in the art of oratory. For this he received training in Rome under Palaemon. For about the first 30 years he lived in Spain. He lost his wife and son very prematurely. This event was so tragic to him that he left teaching profession and found some solace and peace in studies and writings. He accepted Cicero as his model. He wrote a famous book entitled "Institute of Oratory" (Institution Oratoria), which was published in twelve volumes. This work has been regarded as a great contribution to education made by Romans. This book explains the art of giving speech and the methods of teaching various subjects.

IMPORTANCE OF QUINTILLIAN

From the point of view of education, Quintillian occupies a very important place among Roman thinkers, because we can easily have an idea of the Roman system of education through the study of his life and writings. Besides, his educational ideas had their impact on education from the fifteenth to the eighteenth century. After the Renaissance in the Western Europe, Latin Grammar Schools dominated the educational scene. Quintillian's writings clearly explain their nature, organisation and methods of working.

Quintillian was born probably in the year 35 A.D. in Spain. He received higher education in Rome. His aim in life was to become a good orator. He was appointed as a salaried teacher of Rome. In 88 A.D. he left his teaching profession and became engaged in writing of books. His book entitled 'Institute of Oratory' is worth study from educational view-point. This is the first book of its kind in education given by Romans to the world.

QUALITIES OF AN ORATOR

The various qualities of an orator are explained by Quintillian in his famous book entitled 'Institute of Oratory'. Oratory had a special place in the lives of the Romans. A person expert in the art of oratory could produce in the public the required feelings according to the demands of a social situation. In the determination of the state policy, at the time of war, in the judicial courts and at the occasion of paying homage the great men oratory occupied a special significance. Hence, Quintillian has made a psychological analysis of oratory in his book.

He says that the orator should be on strong character. He should have a deep understanding of human nature in order that he may assess the needs of all. If he is not of good character, he will do great harm instead of doing any good. Quintillian says, "The orator should be good in intelligence, pure in morality, skilful in science and expert in speech. The orator should know the correct articulation and modulation of speech and voice. He should be expert in showing graceful gestures and necessary movements of the body while delivering the speech. His method should be such as to indicate as if the words are flowing automatically from his heart. He should have a knowledge of various subjects in order that on an occasion he may refer to the history, life and ideals of the nation".[1]

QUINTILLIAN'S PRINCIPLES OF EDUCATION

Quintillian held the parents responsible for education of the child. Education is of great importance in early life, as the impression created during childhood cannot be eradicated easily. Quintillian's ideas remind us of modern views on the subject. He had faith in the intelligence of children, but he failed in assessing their capacities correctly, as he has remarked that the children have greater power of physical edurance in comparison to adults. This conclusion made by Quintillian created bad results. Consequently, children were made to memorise things like parrots. This method prevailed for long till Rousseau raised his voice against it. Quintillian has well analysed the work of a teacher. His analysis proved to be very useful for the teacher during his days.

Quintillaian primarily aims at literary education. So, he does not pay much attention on physical education. He thought that the nature of children could be understood through their plays. Thus, he appears to be a forerunner. Froebel who has explained how the education of children could be based on plays. Quintillian wants to organise only those plays for children which may develop their intelligence. He did not like lethargy in children. Quintillian foresees the ideas laid down also by Pestalozzi and Montessori. During his days children in Roman School were given severe corporal punishments. The very name of the teacher was a terror to the children. This had a bad effect on their good tender feelings. Quintillian has bitterly criticised the system of corporal punishment prevailing in schools of the day. But it did not produce any change in the system. It was from the eighteenth century that because of the influence welded by Pestalozzi that corporal punishment began to be shunned. Quintillian has opined that the teacher should teach children through praise and affection. Affection, praise and sympathy are the greatest reward for children. Quintillian has laid great stress on the character of a teacher. The teacher's character should be such as to inspire reverence in children's hearts. The teacher should be a master of his subject. He should be able to organise the teaching work according to the needs of children. His method of teaching should be interesting. He should not be of dry nature. Quintillian says, "The children should be kept away from dry teachers in the same manner as dry clay has to be kept away from tender plants. The children become dry under the influence of such teachers".[2]

Quintillian recommends the teaching of various subjects in one continuation. He thinks that the study of the same subject for a long time becomes boring. Therefore, he opines that the change of subject is necessary for recreation and mental rest. Geometry or music may be taught along with rhetorics. Quintillian divides rhetorics into two parts: (1) the correct method of speech; and (2) analysis of poets. In both these parts writing and readings are included respectively. Quintillian refers also to the principle of literary criticism in his book. In his opinion a prospective orator should acquire a knowledge of astronomy, philosophy, geometry and music. Through music he may modulate his voice. With the help of geometry he may understand nature. Thus, he will become aware of blind beliefs and may try to be free from them. Quintillian was of the view that before acquiring the art of oratory one should possess a knowledge of various subjects. Therefore, he has greatly emphasised the power of memory. He considers rhetorics very necessary for an orator, because its study gives the necessary power to him for understanding the various aspects of particular subject. Knowledge of language greatly depends upon imitation. Therefore, wrong language should not be used before children. The small children should be taught alphabets and words through plays based on toys. The children should be taught rhetorics after they acquire tolerable proficiency in reading and writing.

Quintillian is of the view that Greek should be taught before Latin, because children may acquire the knowledge of mother tongue later. Greek should be learnt first, as Latin has its root in Greek. But the child should not grow indifferent to his mother tongue. Therefore, after some time both the languages should be taught simultaneously. The principle of teaching of another language along with that of one's mother tongue is specially Quintillian's contribution to the western world.

QUINTILLIAN STOOD FOR THE SYSTEM OF SCHOOL EDUCATION

In Rome it was a tradition to engage tutors for teaching children at home. Hence, the rich parents did not like to send their children to school for education. They thought that children contacted bad habits in schools. Moreover, it was not possible for a single teacher to pay adequate attention to each student. Quintillian opposed this system on the ground that children must be sent to school for the sake of their social development. Quintillian argued that the children learnt bad habits not in schools but at home. Children could not be properly educated at home, because good teachers would not always agree to come to teach at home. The teacher feels inspired to teach when the students are in a large number. Thus, Quintillian advocated the system of school education. These ideas of Quintillian had their desirable impact. More and more people began to send their children to school for education. Needless to remark that these ideas of Quintillian are accepted even to-day.

QUINTILLIAN'S INFLUENCE

Quintillian influenced the education of his days as well. But his real influence may be observed in Europe after the fourteenth century. During the fifteenth century the Humanists were opposing the medieval scholasticism. They were in search of a different system of education. They found that Quintillian's educational ideas fulfilled their goals. They found all the seeds of educational psychology and principles of teaching in Quintillian's 'Institute of Oratory'. Quintillian was in favour of teaching many subjects simultaneously. The Humanists liked this method very much. Through Quintillian's book they came to realise how much importance people in the ancient days attached to correct pronunciation and literary style. In the schools of medieval day much attention was not paid to the teaching of such artistic subjects as music and poetry. We have seen that Quintillian had great regards for these subjects. So he had given special notice to these subjects in his method of education. Quintillian had great regards for the development of the personality of the individual. The goal of education as advocated by the Humanists and the education as prevailed during the renaissance period had been very much influenced by Quintillian's ideas.

SUMMARY

Importance of Quintillian

Wrote 'institute of Oratory'. Oratory very necessary in the Roman life. Quintillian explained the art of oratory. The orator should have an understanding of human nature and various subjects. Good character necessary. Clever in speech and graceful movements of the body.

Quintillian's Principles of Education

Education a responsibility of parents. Importance of the early childhood. Has analysed the art of teaching, has not emphsised physical education, the nature of children could be understood through their plays. He is forerunner of Froebel, Pestalozzi and Montessori. Against corporal punishment. Affection, praise and sympathy necessary in educating the child, the method of teaching should be interesting. The teacher should not be of dry nature.

Various subjects may be taught simultaneously. A perspective orator should know astrology philosophy, geometry, music and rhetorics. The child may be taught alphabets through plays. Greek should be taught before Latin. School education is more important than education at home.

References

1. Preface to the Institute of Oratory, Part 1.
2. Institute of Oratory, Parts 2, 4 and 9.

3

IGNATIUS LOYALA

(1491 — 1558)

His Life

Ignatius Loyala was born in a family of noble lineage in Spain. He was a staunch believer in the Catholic faith. Before becoming a monk, he was a soldier. He got wounded in a battle at the age of thirty years and decided to resign from the army he has previously joined.

SOCIETY OF JESUS

After the Reformation Movement which split the Christian world into many religions sects, there had creeped many evils into the remaining catholic group. Some enlightened persons, belonging to the catholic sect, tried to eradicate these evils. Ignatius Loyala, a monk, is especially famous for this task. Loyala was a soldier before he became a monk. With a view to introduce reforms in the catholic group, he established an institution which was known as 'Society of Jesus' and its followers were called the Order of Jesuit. Since the founder Loyala was a soldier, he laid great stress on maintenance of discipline. Thus, the character of the members of this order was very much improved. Gradually, this Order made enough progress. The Pope recognised this Order by being pleased by its good performances.

ORGANISATION AND CONTROL

Loyala organised the Society of Jesus on military lines. The head of the society was known as 'General'. The General had all the powers and he could guide the activities of the Society throughout his whole life. Under him the General would appoint a provincial administrator for a period of six years. In addition to the provincial administrator, the General used to appoint rectors for the various schools of a province. The rector held office for six years. The provincial administrator used to appoint prefects for the organisation of various colleges. The professors and preceptors worked under the supervision of the prefect. Thus, the organisation as laid down by Loyala was of great importance for the organisation and control of education.

THE ORDER OF STUDIES

The Jesuits realised that without proper catholic education, it would be impossible to ensure the permanence of the Catholic religion. So, they very carefully laid down rules for their institution. Loyala included education in the rules and regulations of the Society. We shall understand below the various aspects of education as defined by Loyala for upkeep and continual growth of the members of the Catholic group.

AIM OF EDUCATION

The main aim of Jesuit education was to preach and propagate the Catholic religion. The Jesuits wanted to bring back the protestant again within their fold. This aim necessitated the purity of character by denying one's own interests. Thus, the aim of education as laid down by Loyala was: (1) to form character and to preach the Catholic religion, and (2) to encourage the people to make its root sound and permanent.

rganisation and Content of Education

nder the system of Jesuit education as organised by oyala, the primary education used to be given at home. was due to lack of adequate number of teachers. The hild was sent to the school after he acquired a general nowledge of reading and writing. Under the Jesuit system here were two types of school organisation, *viz.*, lower ollege and upper college.

In the lower college, education was given for six years. or the first three years the student was required to study reek. In the fourth year class both Greek and Latin teratures were taught. For this the students were required study famous writing of good authors and historians. In he fifth year class the student had to devote two years or the study of higher type of literature.

In the upper college, religion and philosophy were pecially taught. Philosophy was studied for three years. the study of philosophy the student was expected to cquire a good background in logic, ethics and psychology. fter completing the study of philosophy, the student was warded the M. A. degree. After obtaining M. A. degree, he student was to teach in the lower college for 5 or 6 ears. After completing this teaching work, one could study eligion for four years. In addition to Greek and Latin, the tudent was required to know Hebrew also for the study f religion. The student was to make a critical study of old eligious books along with the history of Christian religion. fter studying for four years in this manner, he was equired to make some research on some religious topic or two years. On the successful completion of this esearch, he was awarded the degree of Doctor of Divinity.

THE METHOD OF TEACHING

n the lower college the chief method was that of nemorization and revision. The student would revise the reviously learnt lesson before starting a new one. Each new lesson was revised every day. The class was divided nto two parts in order to make the method of memorization and revision interesting. A particular student w encouraged to take the initiative in revision. At his mista another student of the other group would correct him. I giving motivation, the students were given rewards a degrees.

In the Jesuit system of education the ability and s of the teacher was considered most important. Lecture a prelection method was primarily in vogue. The teach would, first of all, explain the meaning of the passa Afterwards, he would give the necessary interpretati Then he would give views of other critics and writers.

The literary beauties would be pointed out and t lessons to be derived from the same would also be hint at. Thus, the Jesuit educational system was of a very hi type.

THE IMPACT ON SOCIETY

This system laid great stress on the formation of charact This tendency created many persons of strong charact At the time of Loyala's death the Jesuit schools were abc 100 in number. But in about 150 years, this numb increased to 769. Ordinarily, each Jesuit school used admit about 300 students, but some could admit even mc than 1000. The Jesuit teachers under the guidance Loyala paid special attention to the social good. They ma no distinction between rich and poor. Each was free to g education in the Jesuit school. Unfortunately, during t eighteenth century many Jesuit teachers and bisho became self-conceited and began to indulge into mutu rivalries and other lapses of character. Thus, the downf of the Jesuit system of education began. Latter on, t Pope disbanded the 'Society of Jesus'.

SUMMARY

Loyala established the Society of Jesus for eradicating ev from the Catholic group. He emphasised discipline in h organisation.

ganization and Control

e head was known as General. A provincial ministrator, rectors and prefects.

e Order of Studies

lucation was considered necessary for permanence of the tholic religion.

ms of Education

preach and propagate the Catholic religion. Formation character.

ganization and Content of Education

imary education at home for want for adequate number teachers. Lower and upper colleges. Religion, philosophy d Greek, Latin and Hebrew literatures were taught. M. and Doctor of Divinity were awarded. A critical study of d religious books and the history of Christian religion.

e Method of Teaching

emorization and revision. Rewards and degrees were given r motivation. The ability and skill of the teacher was nsidered most important. Lecture and prelection method as primarily used.

e Impact on Society

id great stress on the formation of character. onsequently, many persons of strong character sprang in the society. The Jesuit teacher paid special attention social good. They did not distinguish between the rich d poor.

4

COMENIUS, JOHN AMOS

(1592 — 1670)

His Life

John Amos Comenius the prophet of Modern educatio philosopher, educator and text-book writer was born Nivnitz, a village of Moravia, in 1592. He lost his paren while he was very young. While he was sixteen years age, he could see the serious defects in the teaching Latin to young children. He was profoundly attracted the new educational movements of the day. He believ that education was the supreme means of human progre and worked all his life to transmit this idea to all. Among his great works some more important ones are : Gre Didactics, Gate of Tonques Unlocked, The Vestibule, T School of Infancy and the World in Pictures.

Comenius had profound sympathy for the comm man. He was a great champion of the education of t lower classes. He says, "The education that I propo includes all that is proper for a man, and in one in whi all men who are born into this world should share. these, as far as possible, should be educated together, order that they may stimulate and urge on one another He believed that all children are born to become me and so they must be educated. He opposed the existen of separate Latin school for the training of an aristocra class and demanded that the Latin school should be op for all. Thus, Comenius adopted a thoroughly democra attitude.

COMENIUS' EDUCATIONAL PSYCHOLOGY

Comenius was an acute observer of the growth of plants and animals, the natural activities and interests of children, and the operation of the crafts and manual arts. He formed a theory of the mental life and the growth of child nature and has based his principles and methods or instructions on the same. He believed that the process of natural growth of the child must be the true basis to education. He says, "Let our maxim be to follow the law of nature in all things, to observe how the faculities develop one after another, and to base our method on this principle of succession".[2] He believed that "the exact order of instruction must be borrowed from nature".

Comenius did not have an accurate knowledge of the mental life. He accepted the principles of faulty psychology as prevalent in his days, and failed to understand its inadequacies. However, it is amazing that he has given us innumerable principles which evince his profound wisdom, and his conception of mind agrees in broad principles with the functional view of the modern times.

Senses : Comenius regarded the five senses as the gateways to man's soul. He believed in the old doctrine that "there is nothing in the intellect which was not previously in the senses". He based his principles of method for infant and vernacular schools on this doctrine.

Imagination : To Comenius imagination was an inner sense. To him it was at the root of the child's knowledge and spiritual being.

Memory : Comenius believes the memory could be developed through practice, but he has also stated that before anything is memorized there must be clear and firm impression on the senses. According to him, nothing should be committed to memory without having discussed and fully understood it. For this purpose, he stands for greater use of black-boards, diagrams, pictures and other similar means. He does not want that every thing should be memorized. Only the most important things should be memorized.

Reason : Comenius thinks that reason helps one to

measure and determine as to what, where and how anything should be sought after or avoided.

Emotions and Will : Comenius recognized the importance of emotions in education. Before him no one had considered the problem of emotions so sympathetically. He believed that natural curiosity provides the inner striving after knowledge. A good teacher depends upon stimulating the native curiosity and not upon artificial methods.

Comenius believes that desires influence the will and determine the nature of the character. He has given the foremost place to the will and moral nature in human experience.

Differences in Children : Comenius has recognized some individual differences in children and has discusses how to deal with them in a tactful manner.

Education according to the Stage of Development : According to Comenius, the child should be taught according to his stage of growth. This is one of his chief contributions to educational science. He could understand the needs, interests, and power of comprehension of children at each stage of development. He prepared text-books for each year of the school life according to the needs and interest of children.[3]

AIM OF EDUCATION

Knowledge, virtue and piety summaries the Comenius' educational aim as the following words indicate : "They will learn, not for the school, but for life, so that the youths shall go forth energetic, ready for everything, apt, industrious, and worthy of being entrusted with any of the duties of life, and this all the more if they have added to virtue a sweet conversation, and have crowned all with the fear and love of God. They will go forth capable of expression and eloquence. Comenius believes that man has expression and eloquence,"[4] Comenius believes that man has capacity to know all things and to do all things and that he has a relation with God. He has based his educational aim on this belief. According to him the aim of education is to teach all men everything. He believes that education has the power to regenerate human life. He regards education as the indispensable process by which the children are made human. He wants that education should begin from the very birth of the child and not from the time when he begins to go to school.

ORGANIZATION OF EDUCATION

The School System

Comenius envisages a clear-cut system of schools. He divides the school system into four stages of six years each. Each stage has its own special functions according to the needs and interests of the particular stage of development. The four stages of school system as indicated by Comenius are as follows :

(1) The mother's knee or the Mother School for infancy to exist in every house.
(2) The vernacular school for childhood to exist in every hamlet and village.
(3) The Gymnasium or Latin school — for boyhood to exist in every city.
(4) The university and travel — for youth. A university should exist in every kingdom or in every province.

In Comenius' days no schools existed in villages, and the only instruction available for most of the children was religious. Thus, Comenius was very bold, far-sighted and ahead of his age as regards his proposed school system.

Special Teacher and Separate Room

Comenius has desired that "the subjects of instruction are to be decided each year, each month, each week, each day and even each hour may have a definite task appointed for it".[5] A special teacher should be appointed for each class, and each class should be in a separate room. Texts should be prepared embodying all the work to be done in a class. Similarly, he has specified many other details of organization that were altogether new for his age.

Working Time

Comenius does not like that young children should be required to work for six or eight continuous hours. He wants that younger children should work for four hours a day and older ones for six hours a day. No home-work should be given. The daily school time-table should be intervened by half an hour relaxation. Frequent but not prolonged holidays should be given. The task demanding more of intellect and memory should be done in the morning, and handwork, music, and practice of style and demeanour mainly in the afternoon. All this indicates how strikingly Comenius has anticipated many of the modern practices.

Class Instruction

Before Comenius the system of class instruction was not in vogue. Teachers did not know to teach a number of children in a class at the same time. Each individual pupil was taught separately. This method delayed the progress of instruction. It was the task of Comenius to show how a single teacher can teach a number of children in the same class at the same time. He has explained the method of class instruction by a series of methodical directions. Thus, Comenius anticipated the method adopted by the Brothers of the Christian Schools by over half a century and Pestalozzi by almost two centuries.

Text-books

In the days of Comenius there was no uniformity in text-books. There were very few books, and they were not available to children. Whatever texts found ready were used by boys to learn Latin. Comenius did not like this practice. He wanted that each pupil should have his own copy of the text and all that was to be taught in a class should be found in an organized manner in some specific book.

We shall try to understand below the nature of the school system as thought by Comenius for the four stages of development — infancy, childhood, boyhood and youth.

The School of Infancy

Comenius regards the home as the first school to Comenius has given a sketch of pre-school training from which the later educational thinkers have drawn great inspiration. His small book *The School of Infancy* shows his great insight into the needs and interest of small children. He has not given broad generalizations. Instead, he has given specific details about activities and capabilities of children at each successive year of life. The book details out every aspect of education — physical, mental, manual, expression, social, religious and moral.

Comenius wants to teach small children the fundamental facts of all the sciences. The special function of the school of infancy is the employment and exercise of the external senses, instruction in religion and early social training. But in the scheme, Comenius was very conscious of the natural abilities and imitations of the children. Therefore, he has not proposed anything beyond the scope of spontaneous interests of children. He has suggested the use of fairy tales, Mother Goose rhymes, stories, play, music, manual construction and humor.

The Vernacular School

According to Comenius, there should be a well rounded elementary school for every child poor or rich. All children should be educated in one common school. This was a radical departure from the old accepted tradition. Upto his time no school had been established for the smaller villages. The vernacular as envisaged by him was to give preparatory training to those who intended to enter the Latin school, and elementary necessary training to those children who had to join some vocation after leaving school. Formerly, these two types of instructions were given in separate schools, but Comenius tried to bridge the gap between rich and poor, low and high children by opening a common school for them.

In the vernacular school children are to study for six years their vernacular tongue, before they begin the study of Latin. According to Comenius, in the vernacular school the internal senses, the imagination and memory should be trained together with their cognate organs. Reading, writing, practical arithmetic, religion, moral, singing, economics, general history, politics, the mechanical arts and cosmography should be taught in the vernacular schools. Comenius wants to make the vernacular school an institution where children should get training in all "the arts of common humanity".

The Gymnasium or Latin School

Comenius wants to open the gates of gymnasium or Latin school to all children high-born or low, rich or poor, whether they choose to be in the workshop or aspire for higher than this. The curriculum of the Latin school is to consist of logic, grammar, rhetoric, and the sciences and arts, and the four languages — Vernacular, Latin, Greek and Hebrew. In the languages main emphasis will be on vernacular and Latin. In the Latin school the attempt will be to exercise the higher faculties of the mind. Comenius wants that his own Latin text-book should be taught. The grammar class, natural philosophy class, mathematical class, ethics class, dialectic class, and rhetoric class — were the six classes or years of the Latin school. Comenius wants that every city of town should have at least one Latin school.

The University and Travel

Comenius desired in each province or kingdom there should be have its own university. The brightest students of high moral character should enter Universities. On completion of the Latin school course the students are to be tested by a public examination for admission to the university. Comenius says, "To the university belong those subjects that have special relation to the will, namely, the faculties, on which theology teaches us to restore harmony to the soul; philosophy, to the mind; medicine, to the vital functions of the body; and jurisprudence, to our external affairs."[6] Thus theology, philosophy, medicine and law will form the main curriculum for the university. In addition to teaching the subjects, the university should also train teachers and leaders for the state. Comenius is also aware that research or advancement of learning should also be a function of universities. Therefore, he is in favour of making the university a centre for the study of every branch of human knowledge.

Comenius believes that travel is a great source of collecting direct information concerning human nature and its institutions. He wants that travel should be taken after the university career and after fully forming moral habits.

The Curriculum

"There is nothing in Heaven or Earth, or in the Waters, nothing in the Abyss under the earth, nothing in the Human body, nothing in the Soul, nothing in Holy Writ, nothing in the Arts, nothing in Economy, nothing in Polity, nothing in the Church of which the little candidates of wisdom shall be wholly ignorant."[7] Thus, Comenius wants to make the curriculum encyclopaedic in scope. However, he does not want that all the details of each subject should be mastered. He has recommended that only the outlines or the principal ideas should be mastered at first. He believes that by a careful grading and suitable methods the pupils may be stimulated to learn more than what the schools may teach actually.

As regards language, Comenius wants to give less attention to Latin, Greek and Hebrew and more to the vernacular. He has advocated the study of modern foreign languages "for the sake of holding interviews with neighbours". He is not in favour of teaching classical writers in the school, because he thinks that moral and spiritual welfare of the pupils will be better furthered by diverting their attention to the study of more worthwhile subjects. He says about classical writers, "If we wish our schools to be truly Christian schools, the crowd of Pagan writers must be removed from them... Our zeal in this matter is caused by our love of God and of man; for we see that the chief schools profess Christ in name only, but hold in highest esteem writers like Terrace, Plautus, Cicero, Ovid, Catullus and Tibullus. The result of this is that we know the world better than we know Christ".[8]

Comenius wants that the Latin language and the vernacular should be used in learning grammar, rhetoric, dialectic, arithmetic, geometry, astronomy, music, physics, chronology, geography, history, religion and morals. Comenius has insisted that manual arts and industry should be included in the curriculum of the vernacular school. This insistence was highly instructive. Comenius has also favoured plenty of physical activity and play for the sake of happiness and health. This was the most revolutionary suggestion for his age. Quite contrary to the beliefs of puritanic theologians, Comenius rightly thought the play life of the child as "nature's method of building a healthy, vigorous body and a normal, keen mind. Therefore, Comenius is a great advocate of introducing of all the play activities in the school life.

Comenius wants to make humour as a means of education. He has declared that the children "ought to be taught, and that thoroughly, to understand what is said in a joke". He wants that the humour should be used for sharpening the intellect of the child. Previous to Comenius no other educator had shown such an insight.

Comenius likes to teach everything for its usefulness in life. Nothing should be learned solely for its value at school, but for low use in life... However, this does not imply that he was a low utilitarian. By the term "useful" and "practical", he understands "use in this world and in the world to come".[9]

THE METHODS OF INSTRUCTION

Comenius may be regarded as the actual founder of the modern methods of instruction. Comenius has become the founder as a reaction against the methods used in the schools of his early days which were "so severe that schools were looked on as terrors for boys and slaughter-houses of minds in which the great number of students had contracted a dislike for learning. For five, ten or more years they detained the mind over matters that could be mastered in one. What could have been gently instilled into the intellect, was violently impressed upon it, nay rather stuffed and flogged into it".

Comenius wanted to impart instruction "surely and thoroughly, certainly and clearly, and easily and pleasantly".[10] Therefore, he has carefully analyzed the principles that will help in achieving this result. Accordingly, he has prescribed certain rules of teaching which may be stated as below:

(1) Natural interests of children should receive the primary consideration. Nothing should be taught to them which is not in any way related with their spontaneous interests.
(2) Whatever is to be taught must be presented directly before the child. No round-about explanation should be used.
(3) It is after explaining the general principles that the details should be considered.
(4) The teacher should not proceed further unless the topic in hand is thoroughly mastered by the pupils.
(5) Inter-relations and distinctions should be pointed out so that the knowledge may be clear.
(6) Things of practical application in life should be given a primary place in education.
(7) Things should be taught in due succession, and only one thing should be taught at a time.
(8) The teacher should proceed from he known to the unknown.

(9) Senses, imagination, understanding and memory should be exercised daily in instruction.
(10) Children should learn to do by doing.
(11) Order positions, and connection of objects should be studied.
(12) Instruction to be given should be within the reach of comprehension-power of the child.
(13) Words must not be repeated.
(14) Objects, things and actions should be associated with the vernacular words.
(15) Whatever is learned should be told by one pupil to another so that no knowledge may remain unused. Comenius wants to encourage pupils to tell others what they have learned, because he believes that teaching others is an excellent device for clarifying and fixing what one is learning.
(16) Materials learned should be properly combined and integrated. Comenius is of the opinion that a number of senses and faculties should work together. The principle of integration has led Comenius to believe that all training gives form not only to the materials, but at the same time to the self-hood of the pupil as well.

The above are the principles and rules of method which Comenius has prescribed mainly in The Great Didactic. He was not only a theorist, but a practitioner also. He tested the validity of his principles and rules into the actual classroom. He believes that the application of his method will make the school a place of happiness and joy instead of a place of boredom.

AN EVALUATION OF COMENIUS

"Comenius was the first educator to develop an educational method formally. He introduced important reforms into the teaching of languages. He began into the schools the study of Nature. He advocated with intelligence, and not on purely sentimental grounds, a milder discipline. Thus a very high place, if not the highest may be assigned to him in modern educational writers. The voluminousness of his treatises, their prolixity, their repetition and their defects of style, have all operated to prevent one from studying him. However, from the preceding account it can be easily concluded that Comenius was very broad-minded, far-seeing and comprehensive. His theories have been practised upon in all schools that are run on rational principles. He has emphasized the spiritual aspect of true education, but at the same time is conscious of the necessity of equipping the pupils for the struggles of practical life. The text-books that he wrote attained extra ordinary popularity. His recommendations with regard to the curriculum though encyclopaedic and extravagant, have been in line "with the new trend of reform in the subject-matter". But his general scheme of reform has not been grately appreciated except by a few ardent admirers."[11]

Comenius advocated a democratic programme of education and stood strongly for the wiping out of class distinctions. But his programme was an anathema in age which believed in the divine right of kinds. That is why his programme could not be acceptable during his age. However, it will have to be accepted that he laid in the ground seeds which germinated into great educational reforms in the succeeding centuries. This is the actual greatness of Comenius.

SUMMARY

His Life

Comenius, the prophet of modern education. Profoundly attracted by the new educational movements of the day. To him education the supreme means of human progress.

Had profound sympathy for common man. Great champion of education of lower classes. Opposed the existence of separate Latin schools for the aristocratic class. Adopted a thoroughly democratic attitude.

Comenius' Educational Psychology

The process of natural growth of the child to be the basis of education. To follow the lead of nature.

Accepted the principles of faculty psychology and failed to understand its inadequacies. However, his conception of mind agrees generally with the functional view of the modern times.

Senses : The five senses as the gateways to soul. These are the basis of his doctrine.

Imagination : Knowledge and spiritual might is obtained through it.

Memory : Could be developed through practice. Memorizing after understanding. Greater use of black-boards, diagrams and pictures, etc.

Reasoning : Tells about what, where and how.

Emotions and Will : Recognized their importance in education.

Difference in Children : Has been recognized.

Education according to the State of Development : Chief contribution. Prepared text-book for each year.

Aim of Education

Knowledge, virtue and piety. To teach all men verything. Education to begin from birth.

Organization of Education

The School System : A clear cut system. Four stages of six years each / each having its special function. The Mother's knee, The Vernacular School, The Gymnasium of Latin School, The University and Travel. Comenius ahead of his time.

Special Teacher and Special Room : For each. Text-books for each class.

Working Time : Younger children four hours a day and older ones six hours a day. No home work. Half an hour relaxation daily. Anticipated many of the modern practices.

Class Instruction : Comenius showed its method by a series of methodical procedures.

Text-Books : Each student to have his own copy of the text-book. Everything to be taught should be incorporated in the text-book.

(1) *The School of Infancy* : Home the first school. Has given a sketch of free-school training, with specific details of all aspects of education. The fundamental facts of all sciences to be taught. Exercise of the external senses. Instruction in religion. spontaneous efforts of child the guide.

(2) *The Vernacular School* : Both for rich and poor. Both as a Preparatory to Latin school, or to some vocational training. For six years. Vernacular tongue. The three R's, religion, mechanical arts etc., to be taught. Training in all the arts of common humanity.

(3) *The Gymnasium or Latin School* : For all children rich or poor. Logic, Grammar, rhetoric, and all sciences and arts. Vernacular, Latin, Greek and Hebrew. Comenius' own Latin text-book. Six classes. One Latin school in every town.

(4) *The University and Travel* : A university in every province. Theology, philosophy, medicine and law. Also to train teachers and leaders. Research every branch of human knowledge to be studied.

Travel after University career.

The Curriculum

Encyclopaedic in scope: Only outlines to be mastered at first. Less attention to Latin, Greek and Hebrew and more to the vernacular. Pagan writers not to be taught. Manual art and industry in the vernacular school. Plenty of physical activity and play.

Humour as a means of Education

Everything is to be taught for its usefulness in life. But Comenius not a low utilitarian.

The Methods of Instruction

Actual founder of modern method of teaching.

Has prescribed certain rules of teaching. Natural interests. Direct presentation. General principles. Inter-relation. Practicalness in life. One thing at a time. From the known to the unknown. To learn to do by doing. Order to be studied. Within comprehension-power. Telling by publish. A number of senses to work together.

Comenius a practitioner as well.

An Evaluation of Comenius

First to develop a formal educational method. Reforms in the teaching of languages. The study of Nature. Very broad-minded, far-seeing and comprehensive. Emphasized the spiritual aspect of true education. The pupils to be equipped for struggles of life as well.

Advocate of a democratic programme of education.

References

1. Keatinge, M.W. : *The Great Didactic of John Amos Comenius*, p. 418, Adom and Charles Black, London, 1896.
2. *Ibid*, p. 409.
3. Laurie, S.S. : *J.A. Comenius*, p. 200, C. J. Barden, Syracuse, 1892.
4. Laurie S.S. : John Amos Comenius, p. 200, C.W. Barden, Syracuse, 1892.
5. *Ibid*, p. 326.
6. *Ibid*, p. 409.
7. Laurie, S. S. : *op. cit.*, pp. 199-200.
8. Keatings, M.W. : *op. cit.*, p. 383.
9. *Ibid*, p. 341.
10. *Ibid*, pp. 229-230 (slightly altered).
11. Adapted from Laurie, S.S. : *op. cit.*, p. 222.

5

JOHN LOCKE

(1632 — 1704)

His Life

John Locke was born in 1632 A.D. in a small village situated in the south-west of England. His father took keen interest in his early education and arranged for his primary education at home under his own supervision. Locke was admitted to the Westminister school at the age of 14 years. After finishing his higher education, he became a teacher at Oxford for some time. He left Oxford in 1667. By this time his father had died. Locke remained at home for some time and practised the science of medicine. His continual ill health had grown in him an interest for the science of medicine. But he was not satisfied with his progress in this area. Locke became a personal Secretary to an Earl. Locke tookup the responsibility of early education of the son of the Earl. In this job he came to realise the defects of the prevailing education system. He remained in France for four years because of his ill health. His temporary stay in France gave him an opportunity to study serious subjects. Locke died in 1704.

Locke has written books in the areas of political science, philosophy, economics and education. In 1690, he published his famous essay entitled 'Concerning Human Learning'. After this, he published two essays on his political ideas. In 1693, his essay entitled 'Some Thoughts Concerning Education' was published. Herein he explained his educational views in detail. After his death some of his friends got his other writing published. His book '*Conduct of Understanding*' occupies a special place amongst these.

HIS PRINCIPLES OF EDUCATION

John Locke has been respected more in Europe than in his own country, England. He was a follower of the principle of acquiring knowledge through one's own sense-experience. Locke was not a traditionalist. He gives main place to 'reason' in life. That is why in his educational principles we find little mention of the development of tender feelings. Locke was an individualist. He considers man free by nature. The State has no voice before the individual. The State is only the guardian of the rights of the individual. This individualism advocated by Locke had its inevitable impact on his principles of education.

Locke thinks that it is not the duty of the State to provide for education. The parents are responsible for education of their children. But according to individualism even the parents cannot force the children to receive education. Locke gives a good logic in this connection. He thinks that the child is not fully developed to direct his own growth. His parents can understand better as to what will further his desirable development. Therefore, the children should act according to the parents as whatever the latter do will always be in their best interests. Because of his individualism, Locke considers every one as equal. He thinks that the differences found in individuals are because of the different types of education received by them. He thinks that we can only utilize whatever nature has endowed to us. Of course, we have to try not to imbibe any undesirable trait.

Locke was not aware of the ideals of an individual to acquire good ways of living. He wants to give him some knowledge in order to further his mental development. He is also careful about the physical development of the individual. He wants to develop the body and mind of the individual in such a manner as to make him a member of the visualized society. Thus, the aim of education according to Locke was to ensure physical, social and mental development of the individual. About physical education, Locke says, 'Pure air, exercise, rest, simple food, are necessary. Wine should be shunned. Neither very light, nor very warm clothes should be used. The head and feet should be kept within the reasonable temperature.' Today we cannot agree with all the laws of health as advocated by Locke. But it will have to be admitted that he attracted the attention of the people towards the necessity of acquiring good health for developing a good rational power.

Locke advises to be especially careful about mental development of the child. From the very beginning, the children should be given such education which may foster their mental development. To Locke only that is education which improves the mind. In each and every activity of the child, it should be seen as to how the same will influence his mind. What ideas will the child acquire thereby? What will be their effects when he grows up? Will the education given to him be his future guide? It is quite natural for Locke to think in this manner as he believed in individualism. But we cannot agree with his views in this connection: Locke concentrates only on the individual. 'Matter' and 'Knowledge' did not have any special significance for him. He closed his eyes towards the social good. Motaigne too, was an individualist in this sense. Locke was not at all concerned with general human nature. He thought only of the special characteristics of the individual. He considers each child different from the other. So, a single method of teaching cannot be used for teaching all the children. Generally, schools do not pay any attention on individual characteristics. Hence, Locke had no sympathy with the Public Schools of the day. He opines that for each child a teacher should be appointed at home.

Locke considers the child as ignorant, because he thinks that he (child) is not yet developed mentally adequately. Therefore, he wants to prepare him for the acquisition of reason. For this he regards sound health and good habits as necessary. The reason is not developed during childhood. Therefore, we can only try to develop good habits during childhood. Locke believed that it was through reason that truth could be recognised. Reason cannot be developed through disorganised knowledge. The teacher thinks that imparting of some knowledge is necessary, otherwise, how will the child pass the examination? Locke says that this type of knowledge cannot develop reason, because through this knowledge the individual has learnt only to repeat or write what he has already memorised. Like Rabelais and Montaigne Locke wanted to develop the individual fully. He did not aim at making him a gentleman. Rabelais wanted that the individual should acquire some knowledge about things, Montaigne paid more attention on development rather than on teaching. He wanted to teach the individual the art of living. Locke, too, wanted this. In those days the study of Greek and Latin was greatly emphasised. This tendency did not educate one in the art of living. Therefore, like Montaigne, Locke was against the teaching of Latin and Greek. Locke wanted to acquaint the child with virtue, reason, ethics and general knowledge. But he thinks about all these in connection with a gentleman alone.

LOCKE : AN ADVOCATE OF UTILITARIANISM

Now we shall see what types of knowledge Locke wanted to give to the child. Locke considers knowledge as a matter of inner experiences of the mind. We cannot get true knowledge of a thing unless we acquire its actual experience. By listening to what others are repeating cannot give knowledge. Carlyle also says, "You have to see with your own eyes". But this is not always possible. Sometimes we have to accept the experience of others as well. We cannot go ahead, if we do not do this. Therefore, Locke says, "We do not mean knowledge of various things, by knowledge we mean only the truth determined by our intelligence". It is through the eyes of the mind that we can experience truth, Locke wanted to give the child only useful education. The education which did not fulfil any self-interest had little importance to Locke. Locke observes,

"We must know what benefit will be accrued by the study of a certain subject and what its effect will be on the mind." Herbert Spencer, too, thought that the best education could be received only by learning most useful things. The one who is interested in utilitarianism often ignores the impact of a certain thing on the body and mind. If education is useful and fulfils some immediate purpose, it is good. The knowledge of useful things should be acquired at earliest, no matter how it affects the body.

In his book on education entitled '*Thoughts Concerning Education*', Locke says that it is from the point of view of individual benefit that we have to judge the utility or otherwise of a certain thing. For the achievement of this goal, Locke has tried to show the 'shortest cut'. It appears that the purpose of Locke had been only to acquire knowledge. Evidently, he was a staunch advocate of utilitarianism. Locke did not like to give intellectual education to the child. To him intellectual education was useful only to that person who could teach himself, in other words, who could himself discriminate between good and bad, truth and falses knowledge and ignorance. We may remark here that if educational psychology and science during the days of Locke had developed to the same extent as they are today, Locke's educational ideas would have been more liberal and useful.

THE CONTENT OF EDUCATION ACCORDING TO LOCKE

Locke was not in sympathy with the humanistic system of education in which greater attention was paid to the study of Roman and Greek languages, literature and civilization. Locke says, "It is necessary to be able to read and write. But this should not be the main thing. Those who have a tendency to read are benefited, but others do not derive any good from it". Locke wanted the proper use of the power of initiative, independent views, power of observation and reason. For this, he wanted to initiate a new system of education. He did not like to teach language with the help of grammar. He advised that language should be taught through conversation. Locke agreed with Bacon that all knowledge is acquired through experience. He did not believe in the power of imitation. Therefore, in the content of education he stands for the inclusion of only those subjects in which the experience of the individual may predominate. For example, in the content, special place was given to science, geography, astronomy, mathematics, Bible and history. In order to explain the accounts of agriculture, the teaching of elementary arithmetic was considered necessary. For mutual negotiation and exchange of ideas, the study of mother tongue and modern language was given a place. Greek was excluded from the education of a gentleman. Teaching of Latin with the help of grammar was not considered as correct. Locke wanted to teach Latin through the knowledge of the mother tongue. Latin was considered a means, and not an end. Locke considers mathematics superior to Logic, because in mathematics he finds a greater logicalness in the underlying ideas. Locke believed that the children could not derive much benefit from the study of Logic and rhetorics. He did not think that memory was improved through the study of grammar and logic. In fact, the power of memory is sharpened by sound health and sound mind. Any special exercise is not necessary for sharpening the power of memory. We are practising it all the time in our daily life. Therefore, it is being sharpened automatically in ratio of our health of body and mind.

LOCKE A REPRESENTATIVE OF THE DISCIPLINARY CONCEPTION OF EDUCATION

Locke is of the view that education in one subject has little effect on another. The learning of one language may adversely affect the learning of another. In connection with moral education, Locke lays great stress on the formation of habits. Habit is formed through exercise. Locke has no hesitation in exercising body and mind for formation of habits. He says, "The power of body and mind lies in going through hardships. It is in the denial of one's desires that lies the root of all virtues". If education is given through the help of habits, the child will easily learn many useful things. The child is encouraged through examples. If he gets into the habit of doing a good thing, he is all the more encouraged.

Locke wants that the child should follow the universally accepted social system. He does not want to bring any change in it. Locke observes, "It is not the function of that gentleman to show any desire for social duty and desire who is already overloaded with traditions". Locke appears to be very narrow minded here. If for education of the child, we depend only on his habits, he will not make any progress. He will not develop a power of initiative. Fitche is against Locke when he says that to form habit is to court failure. Rousseau also says that only habit that the child will form is the forming of no habit at all. Therefore, we cannot consider Locke a naturalist like Rousseau, because he bases reason on habits. Locke believes that under the guidance of good teachers, habits may be formed in children at home. He wants the child to form habits through self-control by suppressing his natural desires. Thus, to Locke, the whole of education is a discipline. Therefore, some regards Locke as a representative of disciplinary conception of education.

LOCKE AN ADVOCATE OF PRACTICALNESS

Locke wants to make the individual skilful in some handicraft. For example, gardening, agriculture and carpentry may be chosen for this purpose. These will teach the individual practicalness. This will be helpful to their good health as well. Rousseau, too, wanted to teach some skill to the child at the appropriate stage of development. During the days of Locke, travelling abroad was considered necessary for the education of a gentleman. Hence, he too, like Montaigne, stands for travelling abroad.

LOCKE ON EDUCATION OF POOR CHILDREN

At the age of 64 years Locke accepted the post of a commissioner in the Government trade department. It is during his tenure of this service that he prepared a plan of education for poor children. This plan could never be implemented. But his ideas throw some light on the tendency in those days. Due to the Parliament Act, many work-houses were established in 1722. Possibly, Locke might have been encouraged by this. But almost all the work-houses were worse than prisons. Locke says that the children of poor people waste their time. They are a burden on their parents. Their energy is being wasted for want of any suitable provision for them. They remain unemployed for the first 13 or 14 years of their age. Therefore, in each Parish a work-house should be established. This work-house will accommodate children of over 3 or 4 years of age. Teachers will educate them in useful arts so that they may earn their bread in future by serving the society. Locke should not be blamed for this narrow outlook, as his views in this connection represent the general tendency of the period. However, it will have to be admitted that the condition of poor children would have been much better in work-houses than what it were in their parents' home. Any way, it may be remarked that Locke maintained a distinction between the rich' and poor. He had little sympathy with the poor. In this respect, he appears to be far way from Comenius.

LOCKE AND OTHER EDUCATORS

Some critics are of the view that educators like Rabelais, Montaigne, Locke and Rousseau form their own separate individual schools. Some consider Locke a naturalist and finds him nearer to Rousseau like Herbart, Locke believed that desires are controlled by ideas. Locke wants to influence the behaviour of the child. Like Bacon and Comenius, Locke makes no mention of natural sciences. Bacon and Comenius emphasize 'matter' and Locke lays strees on 'method'. Both Montaigne and Locke lay great importance on the education of character. Both support teaching at home and travelling abroad. Both decry the system of rote learning. Both dislike unpracticalness of Latin. Both want to introduce utilitarianism in education.

But both differ regarding the needs for life. Both define 'virtue' differently. Rousseau's writings indicate that he was influenced by Locke upto some extent. Both Rousseau and Locke attached great importance to good health. Both were against corporal punishment and wanted to make the method of education interesting. Both did not attach much importance to books in the education of the child. Rousseau wanted to keep the child away from the control of parents and of society. Locke wanted to keep the child under the strict control of the parents from the very beginning. Thus, both are theoretically opposed to each other. Hence, Locke cannot be regarded as a naturalist like Rousseau.

A CRITICISM

Locke's disciplinary conception of education relates only to the individual. Locke was not at all concerned with the personal desires of the child. His system of education may benefit only bright children. Normal children are not likely to benefit from the same. Locke ignored the social good. During the nineteenth century with the acceptance of universal and scientific education inadeqacies of Locke's views appeared on the surface.

SUMMARY

His Principle of Education

Knowledge by one's own experience, search of 'truth' through 'rason'. Development of tender feelings ignored. Impact of individualism. Locke of universalness in his principles. Education not a responsibility of the State. Parents responsible for education.

Locke does not preach high ideals. Attention on physical education. Useful education. Interest in the peculiarities of the individual. All the children not of the same nature. A teacher for each child at home.

The child is ignorant, sound health and good habits. To teach the art of living. Not to make him a learned man. Locke thinks only about the education of a gentleman.

An Advocate of Utilitarianism

Knowledge an inner experience of the mind. To learn useful things.

Content of Education

Power of initiative, independent thinking, power of observation and good use of reason. Language not to be taught through grammar. Content to be experience centred. Learning of Greek not necessary. The study of Latin through the mother tongue. Power of memorization dependent on sound health.

A Representative of Disciplinary Conception of Education

A subject has little effect on another. Formation of habits necessary for moral development. Mind and body should undergo hardships. To place examples before children. To practise self-control.

Practicalness

Gardening, agriculture, carpentry and travelling abroad for a gentleman.

Education of the poor according to Locke.

Locke compared with Rousseau, Herbart, Bacon, Comenius and Montaigne.

A Criticism

Individualist. For education of the bright children. Ignored the social good

6

ROUSSEAU, JEAN JACQUES

(1712 — 1778)

His Life

It is almost impossible to overemphasize the influence of Rousseau on the course of modern civilization. He has revolutionized our thinking in several ways. He has introduced a new theory and practice of education. His writings on religion, society, marriage and government had a profound influence on the prevailing ideas of his day.

Jean Jacques Rousseau was born of a highly respectable parentage in the city of Geneva in 1712. His father was a French watch-maker. Rousseau lost his mother soon after his birth. So he was entrusted to the care of his easy-going aunt. His father was careless. Consequently, Rousseau was not checked from falling into bad habits during his childhood days.

In youth, Rousseau was not able to adjust himself socially and vocationally. He had a mystical attachment to nature, an abnormal sex consciousness and a great yearning for personal freedom. Inspite of his various eccentricities and personal awkwardness, he was able to establish good relations with the leaders of the Enlightenment, Voltaire, Diderot and others. All the writings of Rousseau are deeply coloured by his own experiences. The most important works on which his fame rests are: The Social Contract, The New Heloise, The Emile and the Confessions. Inspite of his great reputation and services to humanity, his last days were not happy. He died in poverty, in solitude and in exile.

ROUSSEAU'S POLITICAL AND SOCIAL THEORIES

The eighteenth century was revolutionized by various ideologies. These ideologies were mainly destructive in their operation. Everything medieval was getting out of vogue. The European social set-up was drifting towards new changes which were making everything old out of place. Matthew Arnold has beautifully described this trend in the following lines:

> "Its frame yet stood without a breach
> When blood and warmth were fled;
> And still it spake its wonted speech—
> But every word was dead."

Evidently, some agency was needed to lead the revolt against everything artificial and out of vogue. Rousseau was quite suitable to lead this revolt because of his personal grievances against all human institutions. "He is, so to speak, the embodied protest of thwarted individuality against a society that has failed to give manhood adequate scope".[1]

Rousseau thought that the savage or the original man lived in a state of stupidity, but he was serene and happy, because his wants were few and simple, and he had enough strength to satisfy his cravings. However, it was not possible for a man to remain in this state for long. His imagination generated limitless cravings in him and thus he was led to create a civilization with its artificial needs which are at the root of all corrupting passions and manners of man. Gradually social, political and industrial lives were organized leading to lower and higher classes and thus to slavery, and to the most subtle and powerful passion of man—the love of private property. Therefore, Rousseau regards civilization a grand mistake, and the society the source of all evils. He has suggested the changes that should be introduced for reforming the state, church, marriage, family life and school with the purpose of bringing them back to the fundamental principles of nature. In the Social Contract he declares,

"Man is born free, and everywhere he is in chains". In the state of nature everyone was free and equal and no one ruled over anyone. Rousseau insists that in order to save man from further degeneration the society must be reorganized on the fundamental principles of nature.

Rousseau declares that the state exists by the virtue of "the general will", which is nothing but the universal good. If state does not care for the universal good, it must be overthrown. Therefore, he wants that the laws of the state ought to be enacted only with the consent of the people themselves, and not through their representatives. Thus to Rousseau a representative government is also wrong in principle.

The above views were highly revolutionary for the eighteenth century and they were a deadly weapon for the existing theocratic or autocratic governments. Thus, Rousseau may be regarded as a prophet of democracy.

Rousseau held that religion should be a concern of the individual and it must not be imposed on him by an institutional regimentation.

Rousseau believed goodness to be the original condition, and evil acquired. He declared, "Everything is good as it comes from the hands of the author of nature". He thought that "virtues, conscience, a sense of right and wrong, a sense of justice, reverence and pity are innate in the soul". So to him the problem was not that of inculcating virtues in man, but of saving him from vices which society puts into him.

ROUSSEAU GAVE RISE TO A NEW EDUCATION

During the eighteenth century numerous erroneous and misleading assumption guided the education of the child. The child was considered as a miniature adult. Therefore, he was taught the duties of adult irrespective of his natural inclinations. Education was conceived as a means for developing certain habits, skills and attitudes in the child so that he may accept the products of the race and civilization as passed on to him by the school.

Rousseau rendered a great service by demolishing this

false system of education. He made the child the centre of education. He says, "We never know how to put ourselves in the place of children. We do not enter into their ideas, but we ascribe to them our own". He made the stages of human development—infancy, childhood, boyhood and youth as the basis of the new pedagogy. To him the teaching and training do not consist in inculcating ideas and skill in the child, but in offering the child opportunities for full bodily and mental activities as natural for each stage of development.

Another ideas on which Rousseau has centred our attention is this: "The individual is an entity in himself infinitely precious, and should never be sacrificed to fit the needs of society".[2] To Rousseau the heart of education is the study of the child nature and to provide opportunities for his perfect physical, mental and moral developments in terms of his natural inclinations and ever-developing curiosities as evident at each stage of developing.

We shall see below how Rousseau has viewed the whole problem of education.

ROUSSEAU'S HYPERBOLISM

Rousseau analysed but failed to synthesise coherently. He has appealed successfully because his language is always hyperbolic. He takes an extreme position and speaks with force in an original manner. Rousseau was a thinker and he has given us thoughts of far reaching significance. He analysed different things but failed to synthesise the same in a rational, planned and consistent system. He ignores reason and tries to appeal to imagination and sentiment.

HIS NATURALISM AND EDUCATION

As we have already seen above, Rousseau says, "Everything is good as it leaves the hands of the creator, everything degenerates in the hands of man. This is the keynote of Rousseau's philosophy. He criticised the artificial manners of the day and pointed out that insincerity, indifference and unscrupulousness have deteriorated man's life. He regarded the life of ignorant people as honest and affectionate. He doubted the utility of the advancement of knowledge and skill.

According to Rousseau, nature, man and things are the three sources of education. Rousseau stands for spontaneous development of organs and faculties. This is what he means by education from nature. He has very high regard for the child's inclinations and abilities which are, according to him, different from those of grown-up men. Educators must not ignore this fact. They should not try to find a small man in the child, because what is useful for the adult may be entirely harmful to the child. The child should never be stiffed with isolated informations which he does not understand. Rousseau maintains that the most important task of the educator is to study the child thoroughly from every angle and to endeavour consciously to let the child be at his own disposal in order to facilitate his best growth. Thus, Rousseau made the subject of education an object of study. This is, perhaps the greatest contribution of Rousseau to the cause of education. All reforms in the field of education after Rousseau find their root in this principle. The ideal of child-centred schools and of teaching through doing spring from Rousseau's conception of education as a kind of "child gardening". Here he anticipates Froebel's ideal. He says, "Plants are developed by cultivation, men by education".

One should not think that Rousseau has made naturalism a soft pedagogy, because he does not want that the child should be subjected to any regiment. It is true that Rousseau relieved the child of the harsh yoke of the conventional system of education, but at the same time he put on him the severe yoke of necessity. He wants that the child should undergo the pains and bruises as a result of his activities. He says, "Far from being careful to prevent Emile from harming himself, I should be very sorry never to have him hurt, and to have him grow up without knowing what pain is. To suffer is the first thing he ought to learn, and that which he will have the greatest need to know".[3] Again in *The New Heloise*, he writes ". . . . The most essential part in the education of children. . . . is to make them sensible of their inability, weakness, and dependence, and assume the heavy yoke of that necessity which nature has imposed on our species".[4]

Thus we see that Rousseau demands for the child "a life of strenuous activity, without ease, indulgence or effiminacy."

THE AIM OF EDUCATION

"To live is not merely to breathe; it is to act, it is to make use of our organs, our senses, our faculties, and of all those parts of ourselves which give us the feeling of our existence. The man who has lived most, is not he who has counted the greatest number of years, but he who most thoroughly felt life."[5] Hence, according to Rousseau the aim of education is complete living.

He points out that ordinary education has sacrificed the child at the altar of knowledge. He should be very Highly credited for exposing this fundamental error. "Nature wills that children should be 'children' before they are men. . . . Childhood has ways of seeing, thinking, feeling peculiar to itself; nothing is more absurd than to substitute ours in their place".[6] It becomes extremely difficult for us to enter into ideas of children. "I wish", says Rousseau, "some discreet person would give us a treatise on the art of observing children—an art which would be of immense value to us, but of which fathers and school-masters have not as yet learnt the very first rudiments".[7] In all such passages Rousseau sounds the keynote of real education.

As we have already indicated in the preceding pages, Rousseau stood for a generous and liberal cultivation of the innate endowments of the child— as the supreme aim of education. The child must be developed as a whole before the corrupting influences of the society and cramping moulds of specialization distort him. Rousseau says, "whether my pupil be destined for the army, the church, or the bar, concerns me but little. Regardless of the vocation of his parents, nature summons him to the duties of human life. To live is the trade I wish to teach him. On leaving my hands, he will not, I grant, be a magistrate, a soldier, or a priest. First of all he will be a man".[8] Thus, Rousseau does not want to train the child for any specific vocation, or a definite social position or class. He thinks that the shape of the future environment cannot be foreseen, therefore, it is not intelligently possible to educate the child for the future. Hence, he desires to educate the child to act in the present thinking that if the child is able to use his powers in the present he will be prepared to meet any situation that may arise in future.

OPPOSED TO DIDACTICISM

Rousseau is a great exponent of the theory of "self-teaching". He is deadly against didacticism. He says, "I like not explanations given in long discourses.[9] Young people pay little attention to them and retain little from them. Let them learn themselves : I shall never repeat often enough that we attach too much importance to words. With our chattering education we make nothing but chatterers". The teacher is very often inclined to be didactive and moralising. The child can never feel interested in theoretical things. He wants activities. He hates all explanations and lectures from the teacher. He does not like abstract talks. He wants to manipulate concrete objects. Lecturing is the most unscientific and unpsychological method of teaching. Rousseau has done a great service to education by making the school conscious of this wrong method. But he refutes himself by exaggeration. He has gone too far when he says that Emile is not to learn science, and geometry but to invent them. However, the truth of Rousseau's contention lies in the sense that lack of independent thinking makes us intellectual slaves, and the things learnt by one's own efforts leave always a permanent mark of wholesome nature. But self-teaching should be limited.

Life is too short to enable one to learn everything at first hand. One can confidently accept the truth found out by expert authority after critically analysing it.

IMPORTANCE OF PHYSICAL DEVELOPMENT

Rousseau rightly advises not to depend upon reason alone, otherwise mind like the body will carry only that which it can carry. Man's reason cannot form itself independently of his body. Operations of the mind become easy and certain, if the body is under a sound condition. Thus, Rousseau stands for extra-ordinary physical development and in the early childhood he is ready to sacrifice everything for it. But he goes too far when he says that upto twelve years the child should be taught nothing except the lesson in physical culture. If the child, according to Rousseau, is directed in such a manner, he will be able to invent science, mathematics and other things for himself. We cannot gain—say the importance of bodily development, but to postpone other things altogether for a later stage is dubious. Rousseau does not credit the child with reason. To him childhood is a period of sleep for reason hence it should be devoted entirely to physical development. Evidently, his knowledge of childhood is unsound.

NEGATIVE EDUCATION

Rousseau ignores also the moral and spiritual life of the child. He seems to have admirable instincts on the subject of morals, but he has no principles, and being dependent on instinct for his morals he makes contradictory statements. At one place he asserts that "there is only one knowledge to give to children, and that is a knowledge of duty".[10] Again he says: "To know right from wrong, to be conscious of the reason of duty is not the business of a child".[11] Elsewhere he says, "that the most sublime virtues are negative".[12]

We have seen that Rousseau vehemently criticised the prevailing conception of human nature. Human nature was regarded bad and religious training meant to replace new habits and ideals under man's direction by eradicating the original nature. This state of things had a strong reaction in Rousseau. He emphatically asserted that first education should be entirely negative. It should not aim at teaching the principles of virtue or truth. It should only see that the heart is protected from the evil and vice and the mind from error. Education of the child should be adjusted according to his own powers and inclinations. The child's will must be always supreme.

Rousseau says, "Do not give your pupil any sort of verbal lesson, for he is to be taught only by experience.... The first education, then, ought to be purely negative. It consists not at all in teaching virtue or truth, but in shielding the heart from vice, and the mind from error. If you could do nothing and allow nothing to be done; if you could bring your pupil sound and robust to the age of twelve years without his being able to distinguish his right hand from his left, from your first lessons the eyes of his understanding would be open to reason".[13]

According to Rousseau, all the accepted educational practices were erroneous. To him positive education was merely an attempt to prepare the mind prematurely in order to enable the child to understand the duties that belong to man. He defined negative education as a system which aims at perfecting the organs which are instruments of knowledge. It does not give knowledge directly. It tends to exercise the senses to prepare the way for reason. It shows to the child the path that will lead him to truth and goodness at the proper time when he can recognize, appreciate and love them thoroughly. Rousseau says, "Negative, I call that education which strives to make perfect the organs of our understanding before it conveys us true understanding, and which prepares for reason by exercising the senses. Negative education does not mean idleness—on the contrary, it does not inculcate virtue but it prevents vice; it does not teach truth but it preserves from going astray. It makes the child fit for everything that can lead it to the truth when it becomes able to understand the truth, and the good when it becomes able to love the good". Rousseau's statement appears to be paradoxical and can be appreciated only in the spirit of the age in which he wrote.

THE SIGNIFICANCE OF HABITS

Rousseau does not want that the child should form any habit. The only habit that the child is to form is to contract no habit at all. Habit is contradictory to nature. In his passion for freedom Rousseau says 'back to nature'. Apparently he must be against formation of habits, Rousseau regarded habit as bondage. But he was not blind to the significance of habits altogether. He favours certain habits of actions, such as those of cleanliness and hygiene. He spoke specially against the habits of thought which tend to produce intellectual slaves.

THE EMILE

In the Emile, Rousseau has not proposed to discuss the problem of the training of all children, rich and poor. Herein he has not explained how 'habits, customs, ideals and sentiments of national life' should be promoted in the child. The Emile is a long good tale, partly novel and partly didactic. In this book, Rousseau tries to show how the evils of society can be eradicated by education. He criticises the formal and conventional education of the day and pleads for thorough reforms on natural and spontaneous lines. In this book, he explains how his negative and naturalistic principles can be applied to education of a child. He takes an imaginary pupil, Emile by name, and isolates him from society and keeps him under the care of an ideal tutor from the moment of birth to his maturity. The tutor is to train him how to exercise independent judgment and will power.

Today, it is not difficult to realize the importance of Rousseau's conception. In his Emile Rousseau has hinted at the race in its upward evolution and at the child who through the stages of development is in need of freedom. Rousseau has started with the hypothesis that the child is non-moral and his intellectual plane is that of a primitive man. Therefore, Rousseau argues that the child should be made free to develop according to his own natural inclinations. He should not be made artificial. No pre-mature training and instruction should be given to him. The education of the child should depend upon 'physical environment and inner-nature, and not upon social conditions'.[14]

THE STAGES OF DEVELOPMENT AND EDUCATION

Child psychology was not born in the eighteenth century. No one felt its absence so much as Rousseau himself. Although not a psychologist, Rousseau tries to establish certain things from his unscientific observations. He divides man's life into four stages *viz.*, infancy (from one to five); childhood (from five to twelve); boyhood (from twelve to fifteen) and youth (from fifteen to twenty). His famous educational treatise Emile deals separately with all these stages. He prescribes the type of education appropriate for each period. Rousseau says, "Each age, each period of life has its proper perfection, a sort of maturity which is all its own. We have often heard mention made of a grown man; but let us now consider a grown child. This spectacle will be something never for us, and perhaps not less agreeable".[15]

Rousseau has committed a gross psychological mistake by dividing human life into four stages. We cannot explain a man's life into clear-cut divisions without each influencing the other. Nor can we assign a distinct education for each period without its being correlated with the previous experiences. We cannot draw a line of demarcation in the growth of human individuals. Man's growth is evolutionary. He does not spring up all of a sudden. It is difficult to say where one period ends and where the other starts. We cannot infuse in the mind something at a certain stage unless its seeds have already been sown at some earlier stage. Rousseau proposes to keep a boy away from society for fourteen years and expects that in the fifteenth year the boy would become fully virtuous. Rousseau's conception is fundamentally wrong here. But inspite of all inconsistencies Rousseau has made a notable contribution to the theory and practice of education by showing that at every stage the mental structure of the child undergoes a change and what is suitable for one period may be bad for the other period. Rousseau has laid undue emphasis on the perfection of each stage, but he has rightly asserted that the method of teaching must be in line with the degree of mental development that the pupil has attained.

We shall see below the nature of education that Rousseau prescribes for each period of development.

(1) Education for Infancy

Rousseau condemns all checks on freedom during this period. He recommends country life, freedom, sports and outdoor games. The child has a desire for physical activities. His spontaneous growth and training can best be facilitated if he is placed under simple, free and healthful conditions. No medicine should be administered in his case. Caps, bangles or swaddling clothes should not prevent his free movements. The child should not be entrusted to the care of professional nurses. Rousseau regards habit as contrary to impulse. So, he insists that the child should not be fixed into any fixed ways. The child should play with 'branches, fruits and flowers or a poppy head in which the seeds are heard to rattle' rather than with artificial toys and gold and silver hells. Plain and simple language should be used with him. The child should not be made to talk prematurely.

Rousseau says, 'Observe nature and follow the route which she traces for you. She is ever exciting children to activity, she hardens the constitution by trials of every sort, she teaches them at an early hour what suffering and pain are . . . . Then school them to the hardships which they will one day have to endure. Harden their bodies to the changes of seasons, climates and elements as well as to hunger, thirst and fatigue".[16] Thus, the education of Emile during infancy is to be purely negative and physical. All that the educator is to do is to protect his instincts and impulses from vice and afford him opportunity for his natural activities.

Rousseau thinks that education does not rise from without; in fact, it springs from within. The first education should be the free and unrestricted expression of the natural activities of the child in his natural environment.

(2) Education for Childhood

Rousseau regards childhood as the most critical period of human life. During this period he insists on training the senses. The child is to learn swimming, jumping and leaping. Some training to eyes should also be given by creating opportunities for weighing, measuring weights, heights and distances. The ears should be taught through music. Drawing and geometry should also be given their due place. Thus, Rousseau regards body and sense training as the nearest approach to train the intellect at this period. In firm conformity with his negative education he rhetorically asks, "shall I venture to state at this point the most important, the most useful rule of all education? It is not to gain time, but to lose it". Emile must not study languages, geography and history during this period.

Rousseau wants to make the child tolerable in society at this period. So, he wants to give him some idea of conduct and of property. It should not be thought that Rousseau speaks of moral training at this point. He speaks thus—simply because of practical necessity. His advice is to exercise the body, the organs, the senses and powers but to keep the soul lying barren as long as possible. He believes in the child's nature and thinks that the latter judges, foresees, and reasons on everything in which he is directly interested. During this period Rousseau stands for intellectual training through natural interests. All types of training should be only indirect and incidental. Thus, we see that Rousseau is totally blind to the social life of the child. He is alive only to the tendency of imitation in the child. Hence his knowledge of child psychology is defective. He ignores the conative aspect of the child mind.

Consequently, his purpose is giving the child some training in drawing and music is to make him only more efficient in discriminating objects.

(3) Education for Boyhood

During this period the child should be instructed in natural sciences. The instinct of curiosity should be exploited for investigative purposes. Rousseau eliminates all useless objects and says that natural sciences give the best mental exercise to the boy. He wants to teach the boy the idea of interdependence of man, and therefore, he adds industrial training to his education. He says that the boy should discover science himself rather than to learn it from others. Geography and astronomy should not be taught through maps, globes and other misleading representations. The spirit of inquiry should be stimulated in the child. He should be encouraged to observe the rising and setting sun and the moon during different seasons and draw the inferences himself therefrom. Let him understand the various problems of topography and neighbourhood and find out the solutions.

To Rousseau text-books are of no importance for the boy. All valuable knowledge may be acquired most clearly and naturally through one's own experience. He says, "I hate text-books, they merely teach us to talk of what we do not know ..... Since we must necessarily have books, there exists one which, to my own way of thinking, furnishes the happiest treatise on natural education. This book shall be the first which my Emile will read, for a long time it will of itself constitute his whole library... What, then, is this wonderful book? Is it Aristotle? Is it Pliny? No, it is Robinson Crusoe". Rousseau was too much occupied with his neouralism. He could not understand that the duration of three years was too short a period to enable anybody to learn the sciences through direct experience.

(4) Education for Youth

This period is predominantly of moral education. "As soon as Emile has need of a companion, he is no longer an isolated being". Hitherto the child has been educated in duties concerning to himself alone. Now the youth must be so brought up as to understand social relationships. He should be taught to respect and love others. His emotions are to be developed. "We have formed his body, his senses and his intelligence, it remains to give him a heart". Rousseau shuns all formal methods of precepts and maintains that the training should be conducted in a natural way by contacting the youth with his fellowmen and by directly appealing to his emotions. Emile is to frequent social places like infirmaries, hospitals and prisons. He is to observe concrete examples of miseries in all stages, but not often as to make him hardened. The care is to be taken that the youth does not become cynical and hypercritical. For this he should be given lessons in history. But only contact with concrete things may not always produce the desirable sentiments in the youth. Hence, his conduct should be directed on the reward and punishment level through the use of fables and stories because, "by censuring the wrong doer under an unknown mask, we instruct with of fending him".

(5) The Education of The Girl

In the fifth part of the Emile Rousseau deals with model Sophie or the education of the girl. Unfortunately, Rousseau misconceives the women nature. To him women must not possess any individuality of their own. They should be regarded only as subordinate to the nature of man. He says, "The whole education of women ought to be relative to men. To please them, to be useful to them, to make themselves loved and honoured by them, to educate them when young. . . ." The women should undergo hardships at the hands of men as the later should suffer at the hands of nature. The women should try to acquire physical charms by bodily exercise. They should be taught sewing, embroidery, lace work, and designing so that they may decorate themselves to please men. The girls should be obedient and must be prepared to suffer injuries at the hands of their husbands without any complaint. They should be given religious training at an early age. "Every daughter should have the religion of her mother, and every wife that of her husband". Rousseau does not want that women should learn philosophy, art and science. The women is only to learn the technique of pleasing man and to that end she should try to acquire a psychological insight into the nature of man.

Thus, we find Rousseau most radical naturalistic and individualistic in education of the boy, but hopelessly traditional throughout in education of the girl.

A CRITICISM OF EMILE

All the educational reforms of the nineteenth century were inspired by Rousseau's Emile. The Emile had its influence not only in theory but in practice as well. Students of education have often failed to appreciate its great historical importance. The Emile is not so original as inspiring. Many of the views propounded in this book had already been exposed by Locke and other obscure writers. The greatness of the Emile is in its revolutionizing effects. It was successful in formulating certain current educational tendencies with such a rhetorical skill and emotional fervour that it won the hearts of people and led them to vigorous action.

While evaluating the Emile we must ignore the offensive personality of the author. His character should not prejudice our judgement. No doubt, we find in the Emile exaggerated, paradoxical and contradictory statements. Rousseau appears to be an optimist while he is apparently pessimist. He is intolerant and liberal also. He does not believe in the goodness of the society, but he has full faith in individuals of which the society is composed. He creates a disharmony between emotion and reason while he prefers nature to culture. He forgets that his pupil Emile is under the constant direction of a tutor in quite contrast to his principle of absolute freedom to be granted to the child. While he gives every opportunity to the boy, he denies the same to the girl.

Thus the Emile, is full of inconsistencies. Rousseau perhaps adopted all these only as a literary device to express his views with certain vehemence in order to catch the wandering attention of people. He laid facts bare before the people and asked them to synthesise the same for their purpose. Inspite of many apparent defects in his work Rousseau will always be admired in the field of education for his brilliant thought, and the underlying wisdom of many of his approaches. The Emile appeals to our sentiments if not always to reason, and, this fact overbalances all its errors and inconsistencies.

The Emile for the first time openly emphasised the need of studying the child. It increased, the importance of the child in education. It gave him a unique place in society which was never given to him before. It distinguished the child and the grown up man and showed that the needs of the two are not identical. It increased the importance of sense-training and evolved a new method for this. It replaced the formal, conventional and didactic methods of the time by more scientific and psychological ones. It showed the advantages of self-teaching. It also gave a place to physical and moral education in the educational programme of children. The Emile emphatically explained the common interests of humanity and established close relation between education and human welfare.

ROUSSEAU'S INFLUENCE ON MODERN EDUCATION

Rousseau and Social Movement in Modern Education

We have already referred to the point that Rousseau meant at destroying traditionalism. In due course of time the main features of his naturalism have been midified or rejected according to the needs of the society. Nevertheless, Rousseau must be credited with many important advances in modern education. He vehemently criticised artificial and superficial ways of the society. Consequently, he also opposed the unnatural educational organization prevalent at the time. He praised the virtues of the primitive man and recommended a simpler basis of social organization. He laid down that all the members of the society must be trained in some vocation in order that each one may become independent at last for his daily bread. He believed that this tendency would lead to a sympathetic and benevolent control of society. Herein Rousseau sowed the seed of vocational education to germinate in future. This aspect of Rousseau's work created a close relation between education and human welfare which we have already hinted at. Perhaps, it will be not far from truth to say that the industrial work of Pestalozzi, Herbert's moral aim of education, Froebel's views on the social participation, and the present'day consciousness of the training of the defectives, and of other extreme variations find some of their inspirations from the Emile. Evidently, Rousseau's principles of negative education and anti-social training were pregnant with many issues which have appeared in the social movements in modern education.

Rousseau and the Scientific Movement in Modern Education

Rousseau stood for personal observation and condemned all book learning. His call was "back to nature". This helped the introduction of sciences in the curriculum and today we find the study of physical forces, natural environments, plants and animals in schools and colleges. In his naturalism Rousseau anticipated the nature and geography of Pestalozzi, Basedow, Salzmann, and Ritter, and he foreshadowed the arguments of Spencer, Huxley, and the modern scientific movement in education.

Rousseau and the Psychological Movement in Modern Education

Rousseau was not adequately acquainted with child psychology. Nevertheless, it will have to be admitted that it was because of Rousseau that the child became an object of discussion in educational programme. He laid special emphasis on curiosity and recommended that these should be used as aids for study. Herein he anticipated the Harbartian theory. Pestalozzi's theory of object teaching and Froebel's idea of motor expression find their root in Roussea's recommendations. In this way Rousseau hinted at the importance of motivation, of creating problems, and of utilizing the senses and activities of the child. Hence Rousseau may be called the father of the psychological movement in modern education.

To Rousseau education was life itself and not a preparation for future. It is a natural process which develops from within through the workings of natural instincts and interests. Rousseau was not conscious of the ultimate purpose of human life. He followed only a naturalistic ideal. Therefore, he naturally neglected many of the aspects of human development.

ROUSSEAU'S INFLUENCES ON LATER EDUCATIONAL REFORMERS

Rousseau advocated many-sided developments and training. Pestalozzians emphasized the 'harmonious development of faculties'. Herbart, too, speaks of many-sided interests, Pestalozzi has partially emphasized Rousseau's idea of development of the child's instincts and capacities. Froebel imbibed this view more clearly. Pestalozzi, Herbart and Froebel, like Rousseau meant to provide appropriate activities for each stage. Rousseau made it clear that sense perception is fundamental in elementary education. This view is especially emphasized by Basedow and the Pestalozzian 'object teaching'. Rousseau did not like that the children should be taught the theological aspects of religion. Both Pestalozzi and Basedow accepted this view of Rousseau. Pestalozzi agreed with Rousseau that home geography should be the starting point of geography teaching. Basedow and modern Harbartians have accepted Rousseau's idea that "Robinson Crusoe" should furnish the basis for scientific and practical studies. Rousseau did not like that the child should memorize words prematurely. He thought that this would destroy the child's judgment. Pestalozzi realised this ideal very early but he could not live upto it and his teaching degenerated into memorizing, but Herbart and the latter reformers tried to include this ideal in their principle of teaching. Very like Rousseau— Basedow, Pestalozzi and Froebel accepted the physical activity as necessary for healthy growth. Rousseau thought that motor activity should be connected with observation and reasoning. Basedow and Pestalozzi could not appreciate this ideal in its full significance. It was left to Froebel and to Dewey to carry out this ideal into practice. Rousseau thought that if a child had ability to reason he must be encouraged to investigate small problems of applied science. This principle was neglected almost by all educators except by Froebel upto some extent. Dewey has revived this principle into practice. Rousseau preached that the child should be enabled to combine sense perception and motor activity and to make drawings from models. He gave much value to the crude attempts of the child in this respect. This ideal has been very recently emphasized by Colonel Parker and Dewey. Rousseau reminded the educational world that it is from the vocational standpoint that the study of social relations should be approached. The nineteenth century educators favoured this ideal very partially. Dewey has especially advocated this ideal bringing many changes in the educational programmes of his country, U.S.A.

SUMMARY

His Life

Rousseau revolutionized our thinking. Introduced a new theory and practice of education. Profound influence on the prevailing ideas of his day.

Rousseau fell into bad habits during childhood. Mystical attachment to nature. Abnormal sex consciousness. Yearning for personal freedom. But had good relations with the leaders of the Enlightenment. His writings deeply coloured by personal experience. Died in poverty, solitude and exile.

Rousseau's Political and Social Theories

Various ideologies during the eighteenth century. The European society drifting towards new changes. The medieval getting out of vogue. Rousseau led to revolt.

To Rousseau the savage was happy. Man has created a civilization with artificial needs and corrupting passions. So civilization a grand mistake and the society the source of all evils. Rousseau suggested measures for reforming all social institutions. Society must be reorganized on the fundamental principles of nature.

A representative government wrong in principle. The people themselves to enact laws.

Religion a concern of the individual. It must not be imposed by institutional regimentation.

Goodness in the original condition. Evils are acquired. Hence man to be saved from vices.

Rousseau Gave Rise to a New Education

During the eighteenth century the child was considered as a miniature adult. Education to develop virtues. Rousseau stood against this practice. He made the child the centre of education. Offering the child opportunities for full bodily and mental activities as natural for each stage of development.

Individual and entity in himself. He should not be sacrificed to fit with the needs of society.

Rousseau's Hyperbolism

Rousseau ignores reason and appeals to imagination and sentiments in a hyperbolic and original manner.

Rousseau's Naturalism in Education

Life of the ignorant people honest and affectionate. He doubled the utility of the advancement of knowledge and skill.

Nature, men and things — the three sources of education. Educator to note that child's abilities and inclinations different from those of grown-up men. The child not to be stuffed with unintelligible isolated informations. The child to be left at his own disposal. Education as a kind of child gardening. Rousseau anticipates Froebel.

Naturalism not a soft pedagogy. Rousseau put on the child the severe yoke of necessity. He wants the child to undergo suffering in order to learn.

The Aim of Education

Complete living the aim of education. Child not to be sacrificed at the altar of knowledge. Children to be children before they are men.

Generous and liberal cultivation of the inner endowments of the child. No training for any specific vocation. The child to be educated for acting in the present.

Opposed to Didacticism

Lecturing is no teaching. With chattering education we can produce only chatterers. Rousseau exaggerates by station that Emile should invent even science and geometry. If teaching must be limited. Life is too short to learn everything at first hand.

Importance of Physical Development

During the early childhood maximum attention on physical development. According to Rousseau the child has reason. But as Rousseau suggests, other things cannot be postponed altogether for a later stage.

Negative Education

Rousseau depends on instincts for morals. Makes contradictory statements.

Criticised the prevailing conception of human nature which was regarded as bad. According to Rousseau, first education to be negative. The heart to be protected from evil and mind from error.

According to him, positive education aims at preparing the mind prematurely. Negative education prepares the child to recognize, appreciate and love Truth, Beauty, and Goodness at the proper time when the senses and organs are in fitness to receive.

The Significance of Habit

Back to nature. Habits as bondage. Must not be formed, except that of cleanliness and hygiene.

The Emile

A long tale — partly novel and partly didactic. Application of negative and naturalistic principles explained. The child is non-moral. His intellectual plane primitive. He should be made free to develop according to his natural inclinations. No premature training. Education to depend upon physical environment and inner nature.

The Stages of Development and Education

Infancy, Childhood, Boyhood and Youth. Each stage has its own proper perfection. No clear-cut division in the growth of human individuals. Man's growth evolutionary. But Rousseau has rightly pointed out that each stage of growth requires different types of education.

(1) *Infancy*

No check on freedom. Country life, sports and out door games to be preferred. The child not to be entrusted to professional nurses. He is not to play with artificial toys—

but with branches, twigs and flowers. Not to learn language prematurely. Instincts and impulses to be protected from vice.

Follow the path of nature.
Education springs from within.

(2) *Childhood*

Childhood most critical period. Senses to be trained. Swimming, jumping, music, drawing and geometry. Body and sense training the nearest approach to train the intellect. No language, history and geography at this stage. Some idea of conduct and property to be given. Intellectual training through natural interests. Rousseau totally blind to the social life of the child.

(3) *Boyhood*

Instruction through natural sciences. Idea of interdependence of man to be given. Vocational training. The boy to discover science himself. The spirit of enquiry to be stimulated in every sphere. The boy to find out solutions of various problems of topography and neighbourhood. No text-book to be used, except Robinson Crusoe.

(4) *Youth*

The youth to understand social relationships. Emotions to be developed. Moral training to be given in a natural way through direct experience. The youth to observe miseries in all stages. The conduct to be directed on reward and punishment level. Use of fables and stories.

The Education of the Girl

Rousseau misconceives woman nature. Woman to be only subordinate to man. She is to undergo hardships under the hands of man. She is to be taught domestic arts to please man. Religious training at an early age. Not to learn philosophy, art and science. Her main aim should be to please man.

The Criticism of the Emile

The Emile has influenced education both in theory and practice. Its revolutionizing effects.

Exaggerations, paradoxes and contradictions in the 'Emile' perhaps, adopted as literary device to catch others' attention. Rousseau only analyses, and the work of synthesizing is left to us.

The Emile appeals to our sentiments, if not to reason. This overbalances all its inconsistencies.

The Emile emphasised the need of studying the child before any education is given to him. Increased the importance of sense-training and psychologising education.

ROUSSEAU'S INFLUENCE ON MODERN EDUCATION

Rousseau and Social Movement in Modern Education

Rousseau wanted to destroy traditionalism. Criticised the superficial ways of society and unnatural educational organization. All men to be trained vocationally to earn their bread. Sowed the seed of vocational education. He showed close relation between education and human welfare. All the healthy points of later educators find their inspiration from the Emile.

Rousseau and the Scientific Movement in Education

Personal observation to be encouraged and book-learning to be condemned. His call 'back to nature' encouraged the introduction of science in curriculum. In his naturalism Rousseau anticipated all the later great educators.

Rousseau and the Psychological Movement in Modern Education

Rousseau made the child a subject of study. Curiosity and interest to be used as aids to study. Exposed the importance of motivation, of creating problems, of sense training etc. Rousseau the father of psychological movement in education.

Education life itself. Rousseau not conscious of ultimate purpose of human life. Followed only a naturalistic ideal. Consequently, many aspects are neglected.

Rousseau's Influence on Later Educational Reformers

Rousseau stood for many-sided maturing and training. All the later educators, *viz.*, Pestalozzi, Froebel, Herbart and Basedow drew inspiration from Rousseau's teachings.

Pestalozzi for harmonious development. Herbart for many-sided interests. Froebel for appropriate activities for each stage. Rousseau's views on sense perception emphasized by Pestalozzi and Basedow. Colonel Parker and Dewey have revived certain principles advocated by Rousseau.

References

1. Boyd, William : *The Educational Theory of Jean Jacques Rousseau*, p. 93, Longmans, Green & Co., London, 1911.
2. Boyd, William, : *op. cit.*, p. 140, Quoted from the New Heloise, Vol. 2.
3. Rousseau, J. J. Emile, pp. 42-43.
4. Letter, 139.
5. Emile, 13.
6. Emile, 75, also in p. 478.
7. Emile, 185.
8. *Ibid*, p. 8.
9. *Ibid*, p. 198.
10. Emile, 26.
11. *Ibid*, 75.
12. *Ibid*, 95.
13. *Ibid*, pp. 57 and 59.
14. Quoted by Hoffding, Harold, Jean Jacques : *Rousseau and His Philosophy*, pp. 141-142, Oxfored University Press, M. Milford, 1930, London.
15. Rousseau, J. J.; *Emile*, p. 121, Cf, also pp. 46 and 122-123.
16. *Emile*, p. 13.

7

PESTALOZZI, JOHANN HEINRICH

(1745 — 1827)

His Life

Johann Heinrich Pestalozzi[1] was born on January 12, 1746 in Zurich. His father, a good physician, died prematurely. Pestalozzi was only five years old at the time of his father's death. His mother was a gifted and devoted woman who tried to bring up her three children under the most painful circumstances imaginable. She was affectionate, emotional, sensitive and generous by nature, and Pestalozzi, too, inherited these traits. The constant examples of self-sacrifice of his mother left an everlasting impression upon young Pestalozzi. This impression led him to undergo all his sufferings, strivings, failures and sorrows for the sake of others. That is why he has received an imperishable success in the field of Education.

Pestalozzi could not learn much at the Elementary and Latin Schools. He attended the higher school at Zurich. Here he became acquainted with the many political and social currents of the time. His two teachers, J.A.Breitinger, professor of Greek and Hebrew, and J.J.Bodmer, professor of history and politics, exercised such a profound influence on him that he began to despise wealth, luxury and all material comforts; and considered nothing as important in life as the pleasures of the mind and soul, and the pursuit of justice and truth. Professor J.A.Green says that young Pestalozzi "whipped himself till he bled that he might be able to bear the pain for any punishment that his ardour might bring upon him".[2]

While during his student days Pestalozzi read Rousseau's Emile, shortly after it came in the market. The birth of his son generated a desire in him to bring up the boy according to the principles laid down in the Emile.

Pestalozzi published his first important work Leonard and Gertrude in 1782. This book became famous as a descriptive novel, but to the disappointment of Pestalozzi it was not regarded as a treatise on education. He published many papers to explain his ideas on education, but the public at that time was not interested in his plans for reforming education. However, Pestalozzi was not disappointed. He maintained his faith in education as a means for improving even the lowest rank of human society. Pestalozzi aimed at making each child and man aware of his inherent powers by producing in him a deep sense of self-respect and dignity.

Most Important Writings: Leonard and Gertrude is Pestalozzi's first important work. This work became famous as an interesting novel, but it could not attract the attention of the people as a serious treatise on education. How Gertrude Teachers Her Children gives a very clear picture of Pestalozzi's principles of education. This is his most enduring work. He wrote several series of letters in order to set forth his educational philosophy. The Swan Song and My Experiences explain the final statement of his views.

EXISTING SCHOOL CONDITIONS

In order to appreciate Pestalozzi's contributions to education we must look at the deplorable conditions of the schools at the time. School conditions during Pestalozzi's days were very bad. The church was still controlling the schools and it was not at all careful to improve them. The teachers followed the old method of memorization. The student was compelled to learn things by heart even without understanding them. The privileged classes hated the common people, and because of the horrors of the French Revolution, they did not like to enlighten them. Moreover, the common people themselves were not keen to get enlightened. Being enveloped in ignorance and superstition, they suspected all philanthropic efforts to improve their lot.

There were almost no school buildings for lower classes. Out of 350 schools in the canton of Zurich, only one hundred of them had buildings of their own, and these too, were not fit for school purposes. The school rooms were frequently used for domestic purposes, even during school hours. Similar conditions existed in most of the European countries.

Teachers were not selected because of their competencies for conducting schools. No special competency was required. Disabled soldiers, tailors, brick layers, tavern keepers and other artisans were often employed as teachers. Sometimes a teacher was appointed because of the temptation of a room where the children could assemble.

PESTALOZZI'S AIM OF EDUCATION

Pestalozzi wanted to change the horrible condition of common people of his days. The common people during his days lived in an indescribable degraded condition because of the feudalistic social and political situation prevailing at the time. Pestalozzi desired to raise the degraded people to the level of humanity. He believed that the sufferings of the people could be removed by properly devised measures. He speaks about his purpose in life thus: "Ah? . . . . ever since my youth, has my heart moved on like a mighty stream, alone and lonely, towards my one sole end—to stop the sources of the misery in which I saw the people around me sunk".[3] Pestalozzi had certain fundamental principles which may be summarised in the following words:

(1) All true reform must start with the individual and not with society, because first of all the individual must be developed for utilizing the advantages of the reformed institutions.

(2) The individual can be raised up by inculcating in him the power of helping himself. Philanthropy should not be considered as a good means, because it robs the man of self-respect. Hence the individual must be taught to help himself and to respect himself.

(3) The precess of development is the only sure means of improving the down-trodden humanity. Every child has the requisite powers to develop himself. But these powers are latent and they are merely awaiting an opportunity to be developed. Education must furnish this opportunity of development.

To Pestalozzi the ultimate aim of education is to make every individual's life happier and more virtuous. He regarded the harmonious development of all the powers of the individual as the sure means for achieving this end. To him education was the most fundamental philanthropy, the first human right. Therefore, he became an educator and social reformer.

PESTALOZZI TRANSFORMED ROUSSEAU'S NEGATIVE SUGGESTIONS INTO POSITIVE REFORM

Pestalozzi wanted to psychologise education and adjust it according to the nature of the child. He regarded man as prone to lead a sensuous life like animals if proper education was not given to him. Therefore, unlike Rousseau Pestalozzi did not want the child to develop at random. He wanted to direct his growth along definite lines, because he believed in the inherent moral intellectual and physical power of man. The development of these inherent powers was natural education according to Pestalozzi.

Rousseau's naturalism is accepted in principle by Pestalozzi in his method of 'observations'. Pestalozzi says in "The Evening Hour of a Hermit" that "all the beneficient powers of man are due to neither art nor chance, but to nature, and that education should be in accordance with 'the courses laid down by nature'. He says, "Nature develops all the powers of humanity by exercising them, they increase with use". Pestalozzi always draws an analogy between the child's development and the natural growth of the plant. He writes. . . . "man is similar to tree. In the new-born child are hidden those faculties which are to manifold during life". Hence Pestalozzi understands by education "the natural, progressive and harmonious development of all the powers and capacities of human beings. He wants that all knowledge to be given to the child should follow a certain order of succession adapted to the first unfolding of his powers at least. Here Pestalozzi is in complete agreement with Rousseau's naturalism. Froebel also accepts this principle when he stresses the innate. Pestalozzi very correctly realized that the traditional practices were against the principle he stood for. He declares, "Our unphysiological schools are essentially only artificial stifling machines for destroying all the results of the power and experience that nature herself brings to life".

The need for developing the natural instincts of the child without any outside restriction was pointed out by Rousseau but mainly in negative ways. Blinded by his naturalism. Rousseau asked to abandon all society and fruits of civilization, and thus he failed to make any concrete suggestion to be applied in the school. Pestalozzi extended Rousseau's naturalism by giving concrete suggestions to be carried out in the schools under all circumstances and abilities. Rousseau thought of only the aristocrat child in the education of Emile. Pestalozzi firmly believed that poverty could be no bar in the physical, intellectual and moral development of a child and society could be reformed only if attempts were made to life every one from deprivation with the help of education. Consequently, Pestalozzi raised his voice in favour of universal education and thus he transformed the negative education propounded by Rousseau into positive reforms.

It was through observation that Pestalozzi wanted to train the innate powers of the child and to eliminate the evils of the society. He bitterly criticised the mechanical memorising current in the existing schools and maintained that careful perceptions could give clear ideas about things. He recommended that the senses of the pupils should be brought into touch with outer objects and that the pupils should be made conscious of the impressions produced thereby. He wanted that subjects should be analysed into their minutest elements of 'ABC', and that these elements should be trained by graded exercises. Pestalozzi rightly realised that 'experiences' must be clearly expressed in words. He, therefore, in the summary of "How Gertrude Teaches Her Children" connects language with observation in all instructions.

One can easily exaggerate the work of this saintly reformer of Switzerland. We do not love Pestalozzi for his originality nor for the success he attained in his field. His greatness lay in his successful attempt of making positive the suggestions offered by Rousseau and in putting them into practice in schools. Even here he was not always successful. He sometimes failed in carrying out his own principles. He became impracticable and inconsistent. In language work he was opposed to all verbal teaching, but he committed the mistake of shaping sentences himself for his pupils. As is evident from the educational works of Pestalozzi, he never possessed full vision. His mind was never scientific. Like Rousseau he obtained his ideas of teaching because of his sympathetic insight in the minds of children.

The inconsistency, incompleteness and lack of breadth in Pestalozzi's works are overbalanced by the influence they have exercised on the society and education. In his works we find all the germs of modern pedagogical reforms. Pestalozzi was born in hard times. It was not easy for his contemporaries to understand him. But he never lost courage because of lack of support from outside. To Voltaire, Rousseau and atheism, deism, socialism, anarchy of individualism was the remedy for corruption. Similarly, Pestalozzi found the remedy in education. Like Rousseau, Pestalozzi felt the acute pain of injustice, unnaturalness, and degradation of the age, but he did not satisfy himself by giving destructive suggestions and negations. He tried to make Rousseau's naturalism specific and wanted to make it available to all. In this sense he may be regarded, as one of the greatest leaders of the social movement in modern education.

THE THEORY OF ANSCHAUNNG

We have already remarked that Pestalozzi wanted to adjust instruction according to the mental development of the child. This required a knowledge different from what was aimed at in the traditional schools of the day. Pestalozzi attached great importance to self-reliance and insisted that the 'knowledge' which was investigated and experienced by oneself was most useful. He held that 'thought' must be cultivated by oneself free from any influence from others; 'love'; by one's own act of loving and not by descriptions by others; and 'faith' by one's own act of believing and not by discussions about faith, Pestalozzi named this direct method of acquiring knowledge, thought, love and faith— 'Anschaunng' or intuitive apprehension. Working under these principles Pestalozzi could conclude that one should try to establish immediate acquaintance with the object of learning in order to study it in real sense. Immediate experience of objects, whether sensory, visual of auditory, come under the theory of Anschaunng. The objects may be simple or complex. Anschaunng stands for direct knowledge acquired by the pupil's own experience. It should not be second-hand knowledge.

Pestalozzi's Knowledge of Psychology Fragmentary

Even today psychology is confessedly an infant science. We can easily imagine what the knowledge of psychology was in the days when Pestalozzi taught. Hence Pestalozzi's psychology appears to be fragmentary. Pestalozzi took form, language and number as the basis of Anschaunng on the plea that all the objects have number, form and name. He regarded them as the actual things. To him 'number' and 'form' were the actual properties of things, name being only to make these properties clear in mind.

Rusks says that Pestalozzi's conception that number,

form and name are elementary is wrong, because these are only mental combinations. Pestalozzi lays special stress on the spatial forms ignoring the temporal forms of objects. Consequently, changes and movements are left out of account. Moreover, certain sense perceptions, such as that of colour does not come under the perview of Anschaunng. Hence it becomes incomplete. But Rusks gives credit to Pestalozzi for finding out a ground-work for each elementary subject and for emphasizing the fact that actual experience of objects is of supreme importance in the foundation of all knowledge.

Anschaunng : Psychologising Education

Pestalozzi held that all instructions should start from what children observed for themselves. According to him in the teaching of arithmetic number should be concretely represented. By placing dots on lines drawn on squares of board Pestalozzi devised a unique method to teach numbers. Processes of addition, subtraction, multiplication etc., were taught in the same way.

Pestalozzi wanted that the pupils should apprehended form and name as soon as possible. The pupils were to draw lines, angles and rectangles representing various objects. Pestalozzi wanted that behind all the efforts of the pupils there must be some end in view. So angles, rectangles and objects were drawn to master certain things which were always present before the pupils. Things like sticks and pencils were placed before them and they were to draw lines, representing them. They were to repeat their names till they mastered them completely.

Pestalozzi had the capacity to go deep into the minds of children. From the very beginning of his career at Burgdaaf he wanted to combine the vocational and intellectual training of his pupils. But he could not do so because of certain social handicaps on the part of the pupils. After this he turned towards observational methods which actually started the psychological movement in education. Pestalozzi says, "As a result of these experiments there unfolded itself gradually in my mind the idea of the possibility of an 'ABC' of observation, to which I now attach great importance". He gave the essence of his doctrine when he declared, "I wish to psychologise instruction". By this statement he meant to harmonise the laws of intellectual development with that of instruction. He also meant to analyse the various elements of knowledge and to prescribe graded exercises for them. There were certain inherent errors in Pestalozzi's methods from the very start. Nevertheless, they produced remarkable results which have been systematically developed and applied.

EDUCATIONAL CREEDS OF PESTALOZZI

Pestalozzi's biographer Morf has beautifully summarised his education creeds in the following manner :

(1) Observation, being the basis of instruction must be regarded as the most important one.

(2) Experience and observations of the pupils must be connected with speech.

(3) No attempt should be made to judge or criticise while the child is learning.

(4) Knowledge to be given to the child must be analysed into its simplest elements. It is from these elements that instruction should be begun according to the development of the child. The whole thing must be brought into a psychological sequence.

(5) Until the child masters a particular thing thoroughly the teacher should not proceed forward.

(6) Dogmatic exposition should be condemned, and instruction should be in accordance with the laws of development.

(7) The educator must regard the individuality of the child as sacred.

(8) To develop the powers of the mind should be the chief aim of elementary education. Acquisition of knowledge should be only a secondary affair.

(9) Power and skill must accompany knowledge and information.
(10) The relation and discipline between the teacher and the taught must be regulated by love.
(11) Instruction should be only a handmaid to the end of education.
(12) It is in the relation of mother and child that the ground for moral-religious bringing-up can be found.

Observational Methods

Pestalozzi employed the observational methods in the teaching of all subjects. Thus, children could easily understand the existing relations between things and express them in language. To teach simplification Pestalozzi devised a table of fractions consisting of squares. Some of these squares were divided horizontally into two, three or even ten equal parts. The pupils could thus understand the parts of units and form them into integers. Pestalozzi further developed a 'table of fraction' of fractions. Herein squares were divided both vertically and horizontally. By this the pupil could easily understand that two fractions were reduced to the same denominator. In these processes Pestalozzi and later his followers were most radical. Paper was not used in the work and many of students became expert in calculation.

Similarly, in drawing and writing the children were taught the elements of form. Pestalozzi could not successfully determine the graded exercises for building up form its elements. Buss helped Pestalozzi enormously in this connection. He analysed objects like sticks and pencils into their elements. These elements were represented on the board in shape of various forms. The pupils were to practise these forms first and then asked to combine these to draw the figure of a particular object. This process was also employed in the case of writing.

Constructive geometry was also taught by the above method. The pupils were first taught to draw vertical, horizontal, oblique and parallel lines and then right, acute, btuse angles, triangles and other things. In order to epresent objects before pupils concretely, the figures were ut on cardboard into models. Thus, the pupils were to vork out demonstrations for themselves instead of copying hem out from a book. Thus, the teaching of geometry ecame more valuable and interesting.

In the teaching of nature study, geography and history, oo, the concrete observational method was continued. The upils were to observe trees, flowers and birds and note lown their peculiarities. Sometimes they were drawn and liscussed. In geography the children were to describe some amiliar place after careful observation. They were asked o observe the valley of Buron near at hand in detail. 'hey were to model it upon long tables in clay brought rom its sides. Karl, the scientist, who psychologised eography was inspired by Pestalozzi. Pestalozzi could not pply his method to music, because he did not know much bout the subject. This task was done by his friend, Nageli. Nageli analysed music in its simplest tone elements and hen combined the same into more complex and connected vholes.

Pestalozzi like Stanz, followed a psychological method n the field of religious and moral training too. He wanted o make his pupils realise the existence of conscience by oncrete examples. He wanted to develop it by successive steps. He held that the love of God could be taught better hrough dogmas and catechism. He believed that the pupil should be given the idea of obedience, duty and unselfishness by requiring him to wait before fulfilling his lesires. In this way the pupil will realise that his own is iot the only will or pleasure in the world.

Development of Faculties

The appearance of an instinct or capacity' was regarded by Pestalozzi an important stage in the development of 'aculties. The instinct to walk appears in the child at about he second year. Hence Pestalozzi termed it as a delayed nstinct. Rousseau said, "It does more harm than good to each the child to walk before the instinct has appeared".

On this ground both Rousseau and Pestalozzi did not favour the teaching of history to children before adolescence.

To Pestalozzi oral speech matures in a natural way. Some capacities develop through training, such as drawing or writing etc. He favoured the training of such general faculties as physical, intellectual, reasoning in children. He wanted that the teacher should be constantly working at developing these faculties in the children from the very beginning. Imbued with these idea Pestalozzi advocated the harmonious development of all faculties. The principle of harmonious development bore both good and bad results. It proved to be healthy in calling attention to many possibilities of education which were overlooked by the old narrow curriculum. It proved also harmful in the sense that some of his followers indulged in formal disciplining of powers with materials which were not of any social value.

School a Home

Pestalozzi wanted to create a home spirit in the school atmosphere. The whole work in the school should be so arranged as to make the child feel that he is in his own home. The loving care of the teacher was most important to Pestalozzi in this respect. Rousseau stood for orderly domesticity in the '*New Heloise*'. He was not alive to the Pestalozzi's spirit of love in the school. Pestalozzi advocated that the school be thoroughly reformed through the discipline of a 'thinking love'. This is what he sincerely felt all the time. Once a father of Pestalozzi's pupil came to visit his school and remarked, "Why, this is not a school but a family". Pestalozzi was overjoyed and said, "This is the greatest compliment that you can give me. Thank God that I am able to show to the world that there should be no gulf between home and school".

This 'home spirit' which is so rightly pleaded for by Pestalozzi is very urgently needed in the modern schools. No scheme can successfully work unless the teacher feels for his student. He must be tempera mental so framed as o sympathise with the shortcomings of children and naintain a loving attitude towards them. Only then he an hope to eliminate complexes out of children and eplace them by desirable sentiments worthy of reminding hem of their noble ends in life.

'he Place of Punishment in the School

'estalozzi was quite alive to the need of punishment in he school on the principle on which it was desirable in he home. He thought that it was good if no punishment 'as given, because punishment creates a bad impression oth on the child and the teacher. It might make the hild obstinate. But Pestalozzi realised that punishment 'as sometimes unavoidable specially when the children ehaved mischievously. So, he prescribed its use at times. ;ut if punishment was desirable in home at times, and ne school was to be a home for children; then punishment night have a place in the school as well.

AN EVALUATION OF PESTALOZZI

estalozzi's works lack the scientific precision that we emand to-day. His efforts in education were tentative.[4] ut they are more reliable than many other pretentious 'orks, as he has produced them after great experience. With Pestalozzi it may be truly said that the necessity 'as the mother of invention. . . . It was this necessity 'hich constrained him to allot to intuitive apprehension place in education . . . . and above all to make direct cquaintance with, or immediate experience of, actual bjects and processes, the common starting point of all ıstruction".[5]

Pestalozzi had an invincible faith in education as the reatest and surest means for individual and social dvancement. Von Raumer says that Pestalozzi "had ompelled the scholasitic world to revise the whole of their ısk, to reflect on the nature and destiny of man, as also n the proper way of leading him from his youth towards is destiny".[6] By this unprecedental enthusiasm Pestalozzi succeeded in inducing kings and rulers to take interes in the education of poor children. He democratise education by stating that it is the birth right of ever individual to have his inherent powers fully developed.

We have seen above how Pestalozzi psychologise education. Pestalozzi did not believe in presenting ready made materials before children. He wanted them to lear things through exercise in the normal activities of life Needless to say that this is one of the chief principles c modern education.

Pestalozzi was the first educator to conceive the ide of organic education. He was opposed to the traditiona method of instruction which emphasised memory and th exclusive appeal to imagination. He understood the inter relation of the various aspect of human organism Therefore, he demanded the harmonious development c all powers—head, hand and heart.

Pestalozzi wanted to develop intellectual powers of th child through sense impressions; the practical power through the movements of arms and legs, and the moral religious life through emotions which the child feels i relation to his mother. To Pestalozzi all the subjects i the curriculum should have their origin in these thre springs of human experience.

Pestalozzi revolutionalized the teaching of geography arithmetic, and nature study by emphasizing the principl that the concrete should precede the abstract. Pestalozz held the perception of concrete objects, the performing c concrete acts, and the experiencing of actual emotiona responses as the supreme method of education. H regarded this idea as his greated contribution to educatior

Pestalozzi regarded development as a gradual building up of power. Therefore, he has recommended that no ste should be taken until the child is fully able to master th new idea or activity. From this principle has been derive the grading of the modern school into classes and th grading of the curriculum.

Pestalozzi wanted that religion must be developed fror within. It must be a matter of the heart and not of th head, *i.e.*, a series of dogmas, Religion in the life of chil should be developed by utilizing life situations, personal relationships and actual experiences, and not by the traditional methods of the church.

Pestalozzi has devised a new method of class instruction. Before him the practice had been of individual instruction turn by turn.

Pestalozzi succeeded in revoltuionizing the conception of school discipline by basing it upon the mutual sympathy of pupil and teacher and by introducing the spirit of home in the school.

Pestalozzi has given a new outlook to education as a science. His work at Yverdun was accepted as the model for the training of teachers in Germany, Pestalozzi's ideas though tentative and indefinite have stimulated the greatest efforts towards the exploration of science of education.

SUMMARY

His Life

Pestalozzi very much influenced by his mother. Because of the influence of his teacher, he began to despise wealth, luxury and all material comforts. Influenced by Rousseau's Emile.

Pestalozzi not discouraged by the public disinterestedness in his work. He maintained his faith in education for improving human society. He wanted to produce a deep sense of self-respect and dignity in man.

The Existing School Conditions

Very bad during Pestalozzi's days. The schools under the church. Old methods of instruction still prevailing. A gulf between the privileged class and the common people. The common people suspected any effort to improve them. No school buildings for lower classes. No special competencies required to teachers.

Pestalozzi's Aim of Education

Pestalozzi wanted to change the horrible condition of the common people. His fundamental principles for reforming men :

(1) Reform must start with the individual.
(2) The individual should be taught to help and respect himself.
(3) All powers latent in the individual awaiting an opportunity for development which education must furnish.

The ultimate aim of education to make man happier and virtuous. The harmonious development of all the powers of the individual. Education — the first human right.

Pestalozzi Transformed Rousseau's Negative Suggestions into Positive Reforms : Wanted to psychologise education and to adjust it according to the need of the child. The child to be directed along definite lines. Development of inherent powers is the natural education.

Rousseau's naturalism was accepted in principle. Child growth similar to that of the plant. Education means progressive and harmonious development of all powers and capacities of man. All knowledge to be given should follow a due succession.

Rousseau pointed out the need of developing the natural instincts in a negative way — but Pestalozzi gives concrete suggestions and transformed Rousseau's naturalism into positive reforms.

Pestalozzi gave special emphasis on observation to train the innate powers. Pupils to be made conscious of the impressions producted. Subjects to be analysed into elements and graded exercises recommended for them.

Real greatness of Pestalozzi lies in making Rousseau's suggestions positive. Pestalozzi sometimes failed in carrying out his own principles.

All the germs of modern pedagogical reforms in Pestalozzi works. He could not be appreciated during his life time. He found remedy of all social evils in education. He made Rousseau's naturalism available to all.

The Theory of Anschaunng

Pestalozzi insisted that knowledge must be investigated and experienced by oneself. He advocated immediate acquaintance with the object of learning. Anschaunng is direct knowledge acquired by the pupil.

Pestalozzi's Knowledge of Psychology Fragmentary

Defective psychology of his days. His psychology fragmentary.

Pestalozzi gave undue emphasis on spatial forms — ignoring the temporal forms of objects.

Anschaunng : Psychologising Education : All instructions to start from direct observation. Numbers to be correctly represented in the teaching of arithmetic.

Form and name to be apprehended as soon as possible. Some end in view in all the efforts of the pupils.

Pestalozzi tried to harmonize the laws of intellectual development with those of instruction.

Educational Creeds of Pestalozzi

(1) Observation most important.
(2) Experiences and observation to be connected with speech.
(3) Not to criticise while learning.
(4) Knowledge to be given must be analysed.
(5) Let the child master one thing at a time.
(6) Instruction according to the laws of development.
(7) Individuality of the child sacred.
(8) Development of the mental powers the supreme aim.
(9) Knowledge to give power and skill.
(10) Discipline through love.
(11) Instruction of means of education.
(12) Moral-religious bringing up through the relation between the mother and child.

Observational Methods in all Subjects : Hence children could understand the existing relations between things and express them in language.

In drawing, writing and geometry elements of forms to be taught first. Pupils to work out demonstrations for themselves.

Nature study, geography and history to be learnt by concrete observations.

Psychological method in the field of moral and religious training too. Idea of obedience, duty, selfishness and conscience to be given by concerted examples.

Development of Faculties : The appearance of an instinct an important stage in the development of faculties. The child not to be taught any thing prematurely.

Pestalozzi advocated the harmonious development of all faculties. This principle had both good and bad results.

School a Home : A home spirit in the school. No gulf between home and school.

The Place of Punishment in the School : Punishment sometimes unavoidable. It has a place in the school as in the home.

An Evaluation of Pestalozzi

His works lack scientific precision. His efforts tentative.

Regarded education as the surest means for individual and social betterment. Democratised education.

Psychologised education. Against presenting ready-made materials before pupils.

Conceived the idea of organic education. Demanded the harmonious development of all powers.

Sense impressions, movements of arms and legs and emotions are the three springs of human experience.

Revolutionized the teaching of geography, arithmetic and nature study.

To Pestalozzi development is gradual. Nothing to be taught to the child unless he is prepared to master it.

Religion must be developed from within through life situations, personal relationships and actual experience.

Devised a new method of class instruction.

Revolutionized the conception of school discipline by introducing the spirit of home.

Stimulated the greatest effort towards the exploration of science of education.

References

1. Died at Brugg, February 17, 1827.
2 Green, J.A. : *Life and Work of Pestalozzi*, p. 22, University Tutorial Press, London, 1913.
3. Pestalozzi, J.H. : How Gertrude Teaches Her Children, p. 9, Translated by L.E. Holland and B.C. Turner, Syracuse C.W. Bardeen 1894.
4. Pestalozzi frequently referred to his own methods as experiemental. Cf. How Gertrude Teaches Her Children, pp. 154, 166, 172.
5. How Gertrude Teaches Her Children, p. 89.
6. Quoted by Holman, H. : *Pestalozzi, An Account of His Life and Works*, p. 108, Longmans, Green & Co. 1908, London.

8

HERBART, JOHANN FRIEDRICH

(1776 — 1841)

His Life

Johann Friedrich Herbart was born in 1776. His birth place was Oldenburg, in north-eastern Germany. His mother was a lady of superior intelligence and his father, a Tentonic lawyer, became a privy councillor. His mother took great pains in the supervision of his training and studies.

Herbart was gifted in mathematics, languages, philosophy and music. He showed his various abilities quite early in life. At fourteen he wrote an essay on the Freedom of the Will. He had a keen, penetrating and logical mind. He could discriminate his own mental experience and education. Perhaps, this was the basis of his keen psychological insight. While at the university he came in contact with some of the greatest geniuses of all time; Herder, Wieland Goethe, Schiller, Schelling and Fichte.

He became a private tutor to the three sons of the governor of Interlaken, Switzerland in 1797. The children were of eight, ten and fourteen. He continued teaching them for about three years. From his experience as a tutor to these children Herbart realised that the age of ten to seventeen was the period of greatest susceptibility to instruction.

HERBART AND PESTALOZZI

Herbart is usually regarded as a disciple of Pestalozzi. It

is true that Herbart held Pestalozzi in the highest esteem, but truth is that Herbart had begun his work several years before he came into contact with Pestalozzi. When Herbart met Pestalozzi, the latter was still teaching at an elementary school and had not yet begun his work in the Burgdorf institute and had not yet formulated his educational principles or produced his chief educational works.

Pestalozzi was an emotional genius and had vague visions of truth of far-reaching importance. Whereas, Herbart was a subtle dialectician with great introspective powers. He is regarded as the "father of modern psychology", and the "father of the modern science of education". Thus we see that the two moved in different worlds. Herbart stood in direct contrast to Pestalozzi in the sense that he meant to philosophise education on a psychology of his own.

AN EDUCATOR BEFORE A PHILOSOPHER

Herbart was a skilled teacher as well as a profound philosopher. It was his problems pertaining to education that led to the formulation of his speculative theories. Thus like Plato, Herbart was an educator before he became a philosopher. Some of his chief educational writings are mentioned below :

1804	—	Aesthetic Presentation of the World as the Main Function of Education.
1804	—	Critical Point of the View of the Pestalozzian Method of Education.
1811	—	Several Articles on Psychology.
1818	—	Relation of School to Life.
1831	—	Letters on the Application of Psychology to Pedagogy, the Relationship of Idealism to Pedagogy, Encyclopaedia of Philosophy.

In 1809 Herbart was offered the most distinguished chair of philosophy in the University of Konigsburg, in

East Prussia — most distinguished because it had been occupied by the most famous philosopher stage, Immanuel Kant. In 1833 Herbart came back to the University of Gottingen, where he died in 1841.

HERBART AGAINST FACULTY PSYCHOLOGY

Herbart had a clear conception of the aims of education and prescribed certain psychological procedures in order to realise them. Herbart did not believe in the doctrine of mental faculties as Locke spoke against the existence of innate ideas.[1] "The soul" he says, "has no innate tendencies nor faculties".[2] Again, "It is an error, indeed, to look upon the human soul as an aggregate of all sort of faculties".[3] The faculties are, indeed, "nothing real, but merely logical designations for the preliminary classification of psychical phenomena".[4] Faculty psychology holds that the child is born with all mental powers in an undeveloped form. The latent possibilities of growth may be called as faculties. Within these possibilities come memory, imagination, understanding, knowing, feeling, willing and judgment etc. The faculty theory does not describe precisely the phenomena occurring in the mind. It presents the mind as a bundle of independent parts and separates that which is one indivisible whole. Herbart discarded this theory and advocated that human mind is one harmonious whole and not a confused mixture of many faculties.

HERBART'S THEORY OF IDEAS

Man has certain mental sensations if he confronts certain objects. He becomes conscious of them and acts in the most appropriate way towards them. To Herbart these simple elements of consciousness are ideas. When man resists in face of destructive forces, ideas take root in his mind. These ideas do not disappear easily. They struggle to be upper-most in the consciousness.

Herbart classifies ideas in three divisions, *viz.* similar, disparate and contrary. If a new idea happens to be similar to the ideas already in the upper-most consciousness that idea loses its independent entity and fuses with the old ones making up a homogeneous whole. When more than one idea group together in this way they become more magnetic to attract similar ideas.

On the contrary, if the new idea is dissimilar or disparate to an already existing idea in the mind it also combines but does not make a homogeneous whole. Two similar ideas mix together, but two dissimilar ideas combine together in a distinguishable manner.

Sounds coming from various instruments of an orchestra fuse together and appear to be one because they are similar notes. Similarity of the notes presents a homogeneous whole and it becomes almost impossible to distinguish the notes coming from different instruments. The colour of the floor, the musician and the sound of the musical instrument are three dissimilar ideas. Yet they form a complex whole and they are an object of perception to us as a whole, though the idea of each of them will ever remain separate. The whiteness and blackness of the floor are neither similar nor otherwise — but contrary. The floor cannot be both at the same time. The one is contrary to the other. The one rejects the other. Thus, the contrary ideas are never combined together.

According to Herbart each new idea is accepted modified or rejected in the above manner accoding to its being similar, dissimilar or contrary. Thus the fate of every new idea depends upon the harmony or conflict with previous existing idea. This mental phenomenon goes on whenever something is presented to our consciousness. The process of accepting, rejecting or modifying of ideas in our minds is called apperception.

The Theory of Apperception and Education

Herbart tries to convince us that apperception occupies a very important place in education. He clearly shows the place of old knowledge in the process of acquiring the new. Stout agrees with Herbart when he says, "The main principle which psychology lends to the theory of education as its starting point, is the need that all communication of new knowledge should be a development of previous knowledge. Literature also expresses this view in various forms. Carlyle says, "The eye sees only what it brings the power to see", and Browning, "it is the taught already that profit by teaching".[5] According to Herbart every one has his own world even in the same environment.[6] First of all we estimate the degree of apperception in the minds of the pupils and then try to adjust the instruction accordingly. Instruction is the means by which the ends of education are attained. Instruction will be most successful if it is manipulated to harmonise with the already existing ideas in the minds of the pupils.

Herbart attributed the failure of education of his time to the lack of a sound psychology. His predecessors wrongly attached too much importance to mental faculties missing the significance of ideas alreay existing in the mind. They tried to produce many virtues in the pupils by disciplinary methods without thinking that the pupil does not grasp a thing if it is not related to what he has already learnt. Thus, Herbart proved to us that if something is to be taught to the child it must be connected with the previous knowledge possessed by the child, otherwise all our efforts will fall like drops of water on pieces of stone.

Absorption and Assimilation

From the above explanation it is clear that the teacher should arrange his material in a systematic order. He must be very methodical in his procedure. He must know the order in which he should present ideas before the children one by one. While learning anything new the child mind reacts in two ways. First of all it attempts to acquire new ideas, and then it tries to seek the relation between his newly acquired ideas and the ideas he already possesses. Herbart calls the first process as absorption and the next as assimilation. The teacher should see that he is able to establish a harmonious relation between the absorptive and assimilative processes of the child mind, otherwise his efforts will bear no fruit.

Formal Steps of Herbart

Herbart divides absorptions into clearness and association, and assimilation into system and method. The above four sub-divisions, are known as the formal steps of Herbart.[7] By 'clearness' is meant a clear presentation of ideas to the pupil's consciousness, unless the ideas are clearly presented the child cannot assimilate them. The process which unites the new idea with the already existing ideas is known as association which apparently involves both absoprtion. As a matter of fact, the apperceptive process begins with association. An orderly arrangement in the mind of what has been associated may be termed as 'system'. This process is not active. Herein comes assimilation or the reflection. The mind is deeply engrossed with notions which are beyond the particular ideas just received or previously existing. In the method process the mind attempts to form an organic whole as a result of the above three processes. Language may play a very active part here in giving expression to the harmonised wholes formed in the mind.

It is from the above four steps of Herbart that the five formal steps of instruction have been devised. They are 'preparation', 'presentation', 'comparison and abstraction', 'generalisation' and 'application'. Herbart is not dogmatic about his formal steps. He only prescribes them only as an aid to instruction. He does not regard them as indispensable. He gives full discretion to the teacher in applying his own systematic method.

Rusk on Herbart's Formal Steps

Rusk is right when he claims that Herbart's formal steps are appropriate to the teaching of knowledge subjects. In the process subjects like, arithmetic and drawing Herbart's five steps cannot be applied successfully. Here the pupil wants to do something, *i.e.*, he acquires an entirely new accomplishment or skill. The pupils are engrossed in their work individually independent of each other. The formal steps can be successfully applied in lesson like those in language and history. Where the topics may be regarded as complete in themselves. It will be un-psychological to teach all topics mechanically and un-intelligently with the help of Herbart's formal steps.

HERBART'S ADVANCE OVER PESTALOZZI

Herbart goes a step forward than Pestalozzi in application of psychological and ethical principles in the field of education. In this respect he seeks to complete the work of the latter and tries to remove the one-sidedness which Pestalozzi "in pursuit of his purpose was neither willing not able to avoid".[8] Herbart gives credit to Pestalozzi for devising certain forms of instruction which were suitable to meet the most necessary wants and which served the greatest number of pupils. But he points out that Pestalozzi's devices did not meet the requirements of a complete course of education. On the other hand, Herbart sought to devise means and methods for a complete course of education.

HERBART'S AIM OF EDUCATION

Herbart becomes ethical in his aim of education. He desires that the pupils must be so educated as to possess strong moral character. Herbart regarded his theory of ideas very helpful in this respect. He believed that the teacher can successfully help his pupils to form high ideals according to his theory of ideas.

In the concept 'morality' we can sum up all, the ideals of education which Herbart stands for. Ideals are very important to him as he believes that they lead to action which determines character. Our conscience seeks to satisfy itself about all our action. It regards an action virtuous if it is in complete harmony with its principles. Herbart calls this conscience 'Inner Freedom'. Herbart understands this 'inner freedom' as virtue which should mean the harmony between our thought and deed. He wishes that all the efforts of the teacher should be directed to the attainment of this harmony in the pupils. Constant repetition will help a lot in this respect as it will develop a permanent attitude of preference which must be evidently the chief aim of education. "The term virtue expresses the whole purpose of education".[9]

A virtuous man will always judge the universe from the point of view of inner freedom. He develops a right attitude towards everything. He can distinguish between right and wrong and his inner freedom bids him to behave properly in all situations. To regard the universe according to the dictates of 'Inner Freedom' is described by Herbart as the "Aesthetic Presentation of the Universe".

Thus, we see that Herbart does not regard morality as absolute. Here he stands in direct contrast to Kant. He subordinates morality to aesthetic judgment. It is not surprising then that to him an aesthetic representation of the universe is the ideal of education.[10]

Inner freedom produces efficiency, goodwill and sense of equity. According to Herbart one will be said to possess efficiency if the various ideas possessed by his mind are well balanced. If one can distinguish between right and wrong he will have idea of justice. The idea of goodwill will save him from falling into vicious temptations. He applies his sense of equity if the existing relations between different ideas need to be changed. It is sense of equity which underlies the principles of towards and punishments in schools.

MANY-SIDED INTERESTS

One should cast aside his prejudices and dogmatic attitudes in order to be virtuous. He needs to be very liberal. He should accept virtues wherever they are found. For this it is necessary to widen the scope of education. It should include all the ranges of ideas leading to virtues. According to Herbart if the pupils have a wealth of ideas, many-sided interests will follow. These many-sided interests should not be isolated units but an organic whole leading to a well-defined purpose. Herbart wants that the material for instruction should be so selected and arranged as to produce harmony with many-sidedness. Herbart believes that many-sided interests are the only and sure means to lead to virtues.

CO-RELATION OF STUDIES

Every child has some particular special ability. He should be given full scope to develop this ability. His other abilities should be organised round this ability. "Every man must have a love for all subjects, each much be virtuous in one".[11] Herbart demands that the materials for instruction should be so arranged in an inter-related form as to enable the child to apperceive it completely. The end of many-sidedness can be attained only by co-relation. There should be no dis-organization and want of proportion in the various studies. The subjects should not appear as entirely disconnected, otherwise an unified consciousness will not be developed in the individual.

INTEREST AND EDUCATION

Interest is a kind of mental activity. The aim of instruction is to incite this activity. "Interest is thus a concomitant of the process of the fulfilment or realisation of an idea or circle of ideas by an extension of itself or through action, when this process is working smoothly, not baulked by unnecessary or insurmountable obstructions and not attaining its end immediately and without effort".[12] There is a close relation between interest and information. A man who has informations will feel interest and will desire for more. Interest is created when the mind is not able to cope with an idea tending to excite a new presentation in it. Desire comes out of interest. In order to fulfil the desire, some actions must be performed. Thus interest, desire and action make a complete circle. Interest becomes striking when this circle is broken and desire and action fail to appear. Interest disappears if the desire is fulfilled and the desired object is attained. Thus, we find that interest is apperceptive. We make efforts when we become truly interested. Herbart wants that instruction should aim at securing this type of interest.

Creation of interest is indispensable in attracting the attention of the pupils to a lesson. If the pupils have no interest they will not apperceive any new idea and presentation. If the interest of the pupil is excited in a lesson they may try to enlarge their knowledge acquired by way of apperception in the class.

Many-sided interests create a broad-minded and well balanced outlook on life. Interests have great effects on will. If the teacher maintains proper connection between various interests of the child 'the latter's will, will be automatically controlled. To Herbart 'will' is not a faculty of the mind. It is dependent on the ideas possessed by the mind. In other words, will is a product of experience which is nothing but a result of active interest.

HERBART'S CONCEPTION OF DISCIPLINE

Herbart does not want that the pupils should become subservient to the will of the teacher. Therefore, he wants the pupils to develop moral habits. Herein comes the necessity of discipline. To Herbart, training, instruction and discipline are the three essentials of any system of education. By training he understands formation of character. Instruction is the means by which the character is formed. Discipline aims at producing good behaviour in the pupils so that he may be instructed.

Herbart points out three main striking differnces in discipline and training. Discipline aims at correcting the immediate behaviour of the child in the classroom. Training aims at the formation of ultimate character. Discipline is only a temporary measure whereas training is continuous and its intentions may be realised long after the child is trained.

Herbart recognises the importance of discipline, but he does not want that it should always meddle and place an obstruction in the self-activity of the pupils. Herbart admits that some freedom is also required for the development of the pupil's character. Discipline is necessary, but it is only a necessary evil — because its effect is negative and it mars self-activity. On the other hand, education is positive, progressive and purposive. Therefore, Herbart recommends the use of disciplinary measures when they become unavoidable. But Herbart's conception of training is itself a forem of discipline. Every teacher should endeavour to inculcate this form of discipline in his pupils.

HERBART'S CONTRIBUTIONS

Herbart's predecessors had regarded the training of character as the chief aim of education. Some had hinted at the importance of interest too. But no one had connected instruction with character training as Herbart did. Herbart asserted that it was the moral duty of the teacher to select the material of instruction and devise ways and means of presenting them in such a way as to enable the pupils to have proper apperceptions. The teacher must determine the ideas, interests and desire of the pupils. They must know what interests the child most and what activates them properly towards the desired end. The teacher has to do all this by means of instruction. This contention of Herbart may be regarded as his chief contribution to the theory of education. Herbart made it evident that instruction and training of character should go together. He could not think that one could go without the other.

Now much attention is not paid to Herbart's psychological and pedagogical theories. They are now considered as too mechanical. Herbart had in view the education for adolescent children who are reaching maturity of mind and character. At this stage in life it is necessary to implant into the nature of the individual as many interests as possible. Evidently, Herbart is right when he talks of many-sided interests. Needless to say that he rightly regarded the circle of thought as the surest means of forming moral character.

About sixty years ago, such Herbartian terms as interest, apperception, circle of thought, cononcentration, correlation, culture epoch, and formal steps of instructions were on every teacher's lips. Now they are considered as out of vogue. New terms and ideas are now used in their places. Nevertheless, these Herbartian terms have not been entirely discarded. In their new forms, they are still found almost in every text-book on methods and curriculum.

SUMMARY

Herbart showed his various abilities very early in life. He came in contact with some of the greatest geniuses of all time.

Herbart and Pestalozzi

Herbart had begun his work several years before Pestalozzi did his own. Pestalozzi an emotional genius. Herbart a subtle dialectician with great introspective powers. Father of the modern psychology and modern science of education. Herbart wanted to philosophise education on a psychology of his own.

An Educator before a Philosopher

A skilled teacher and profound philosopher. Was offered the most distinguished chair of philosophy formerly occupied by Kant, the sage philosopher.

Herbart against Faculty Psychology

Faculty psychology does not describe precisely the pehnomena occuring in the mind. It separates the mind which is one, Herbart considered the mind as a harmonious whole.

Herbart's Theory of Ideas

Simple elements of consciousness are ideas, similar, disparate and contrary—the three divisions. Similar ideas fuse together. Dissimilar ideas combine together in a distinguishable whole. The contrary ideas do not form any combination.

Theory of Apperception and Education

The process of accepting, rejecting or modifying of ideas in our mind is called apperception. This theory very important for education. Instruction to be harmonised with the already existing ideas in the minds of the pupils. The matter for instruction must be connected with the previous knowledge of the students.

Absorption and assimilation the two mental processes. There should be a harmonious relation between the two.

Formal Steps of Herbart : Clearness, association, system and method—from these have come the five formal steps—preparation, presentation, comparison and abstractionl generalization and application. These only as an aid to instruction.

Formal steps appropriate to the teaching of normal subjects. In process subjects formal steps not applicable. Sought to devise means and methods for a complete course of education.

Herbart's Aim of Education

Ethical. Pupils should possess strong moral character. An action virtuous, if it is in complete accord with the conscience. Inner Freedom — is a virtue. Education for attaining this Inner Freedom. Aesthetic presentation of universe is the aim of education.

Morality subordinated to aesthetic judgment. Inner Freedom produces efficiency, goodwill and sense of equity.

Many-sided Interests : Prejudices to be cast aside in order to be virtuous. For this the scope of education to be widened. Wealth of ideas will be followed by many-sided interests which are sure to lead to virtues.

Co-relation of Studies : The materials for instruction should be so arranged in an inter-related form as to enable the child to apperceive it completely. The subjects to be presented before the child in a connected form.

Interest and Education : The instruction to incite interest — a mental activity. Interest, desire and action make a complete circle. Interest is apperceptive. Instruction to secure this type of interest.

Will is product of active interest.

Herbart's Conception of Discipline : The pupils not to be subservient to the teachers. Training, Instruction and Discipline — the three essentials of education. Freedom required for the development of character. Discipline a necessary evil.

Herbart's Contribution

Herbart connected instruction with character-training. The teacher must know what interests the child most and what activates him.

Not much attention now to his theories. His conception of many-sided interests right. The circle of thought as the surest means of forming moral character. Herbartian terms not entirely discarded.

References

1. Cf. Lehrbuch Zur Psychologie, bk, ii, div. I, Ch. 1-6
2. *Ibid*, 152.
3. Umriss, 20.
4. Lehrbuch, 236.
5. Analytic Psychology, 11, pp. 137-8.
6. Lehrbuch, 218.
7. Cf. Allgemeine Padagogik, bk. 11, Ch, 1, 2.
8. Minor Pedagogical Works, English Trans, p. 49.
9. Umriss, 8.
10. Minor Pedagogical Works, Eng. Trans. p. 16.
11. *Science of Pedagogy*, Lee B. Chap. II.
12. Rusk : Doctrine of the Great Educators, Chap. X, p. 227.

9

FROEBEL, FRIEDRICH

(1782 — 1852)

His Life

At a very tender and premature age Froebel became conscious of his own inner nature, and he developed a deep and abiding attachment to nature. These two experiences are supposed to be chiefly responsible for the two sides of his educational and philosophic ideology.

Friedrich Froebel was born in the village of Oberweisbach on April 21, 1782 in south Germany. His father was not very affectionate to him, and his mother died when he was only of nine months. Deprived of parental affection, Froebel grew moody and subjective. Naturally Froebel turned towards the phenomena of nature—hills, flowers, trees and clouds, etc., for companionship. Thus, Froebel developed an overwhelming tendency to introspection. His childhood was extremely unhappy. So he developed an intensive sympathy for children which people generally do not feel. Thus, it became possible for him to observe and interpret the experiences of child nature.

Froebel had to make various attempts in order to find a vocation permanently agreeable. Ultimately, he understood that teaching work was the only activity that answered his inner longings. From 1807 to 1810 he spent most of his time at the school of Pestalozzi at Yverdun. Thus, Froebel learnt in detail the methods and principles of Pestalozzi. Froebel did not agree with Pestalozzi and regraded the latter's ideas as tentative, and lacking in clearness and solidity. However, it will have to be admitted that this contact with Pestalozzi prepared him for his own educational reforms.

After Pestalozzi model at Yverdun, Froebel opened a school for boys in 1817 at Keilhan incorporating his principles of elementary education. This school was not success. So he left this school to his assistants and in 1831 went to Switzerland where for some years he conducted several schools. He wanted to devote his life to the reform of pre-school training and in 1836 he returned to Germany. In 1837 he opened his first Kindergartens in the mountain village of Blankenburg. From this time till his death he devoted his whole time to the founding of Kindergartens, the training of teachers of Kindergarten and elaborating his methods and principles, and devising apparatuses for Kindergartens.

Only a few could accept his views. They were not widely accepted in Germany because of their extremely democratic nature and because they could not be understood fully. He was in correspondence with some of his followers in the United States, and he declared that only in the United States his ideas would have full expression. At a ripe age of seventy, he died in 1852.

FROEBEL'S FAITH IN SPONTANEOUS GROWTH

It was Froebel who for the first time applied the idea of unity and spontaneous growth to education. Froebel believes in an internal law which governs all things. He sees a unity in all diversities. To him this unity is the unity of God. God is Almighty. Everything comes from Him. Throughout his whole life Froebel was endeavouring to see a unity in all things. He believed that there was some link binding things into a unity. He says, "Man, particularly in boyhood, should become intimate with nature — not so such with reference to the details and the outer forms of her phenomena as with reference to the spirit of God that lives in her and rules over us".[1] All things live and have their being in and through the divine unity, in and through God. . . . Nature, as well as all existing things, in a manifestation, a revelation of God."[2] Froebel believed that the principle underlying all creation was one. Hence he concluded that there must be continuity in the universe. Accordingly a change or a growth must be continuous. Froebel believes that by the will of God everything develops through higher and higher stages. External interference does not change the creation which develops from within spontaneously according to its own laws.

LEIBNITZ THEORY OF ORGANIC GROWTH

Froebel adopted Leibnitz's theory of organic growth that the seed contains in miniature the whole plant. Likewise the germ-cell-contains in miniature the whole animal. The growth of plant and animal is organic. They have their own laws of growth. Their individual parts and limbs are interdependent. They do not grow independent of each other.

THEORY OF INNER GROWTH AND EDUCATION

Froebel says that to an acute observer the child indicates what he is or what he is to become. All this lies in the child and can be attained through development from within. Had this been true, the ideal of education had been a passive non-interference. Froebel is not right when he says 'that the child, the boy, the man should know no other endeavour but to be at every stage of development what that stage stands for". But this principle of divine unity and organic growth does not work undisturbed.

Everywhere there are various kinds of obstructions which disturb our inner growth. Our original nature becomes very much changed because of the vicissitudes of life. Hence educations needed to check this deviation from the right path. We are liable to fall victims to various temptations if we do not receive proper education. "Education is needed to lead and guide man to clearness concerning himself and in himself, to peace with nature, and to unity with God, hence, it should lead him to a knowledge of himself and of mankind, to a knowledge of God and Nature, and to the pure and holy life to which such knowledge leads".[3] Nature study should be included in the curriculum as it will acquaint the children with the handi-work of God. Mathematics will make clear to them that the universe is governed by its own laws.

FROEBEL ON MENTAL DEVELOPMENT

To Froebel mental growth is organic. In order to make a plant grow we induce it to become active in its own natural way. We may seek to abridge the time or modify the result but we have to act through the plant's own activity. The activity of a thing's own self may be called self-activity (*Education of Man*, p. 9). Knowing, feeling and willing are the three major activities of the mind. Exercises directed towards mental development must be in complete accord with the process of knowing, feeling and willing, and at the same time proportionately balanced according to their strength. We find the result better if the activity is that of the whole mind. In other words, knowing, feeling and willing must all take their rightful share in the exercise, and in particular, feeling and willing — the mind's powers of prompting and nourishing, of maintaining and directing its own activities — must never be neglected.[4]

"A divine message or eternal regulation of the universe there verily is, in regard to every conceivable procedure and affair of man; faithfully following this, said procedure or affair will prosper.... not following this..... destruction and wreck are certain for every affair.[5] These words of Carlyle aptly express Froebel's thought on education. We must first of all ascertain the divine message before we attempt to educate. Froebel believes that this divine message may be learnt by studying the nature of organism. Each human being must "develop from within self-active and free, in accordance with the eternal law. This is the problem and the aim of all education in instruction and training; there can be and should be no other".[6]

In the term 'self-activity may be summed up the

general method advocated by Froebel. To him the soul itself is an activity. To be active is inherent in our nature. With our birth we bring certain tendencies which always prompt us to action. Thus mind is a purposive activity.

Froebel believes that mind is a unity just as life is also a unity. Mind has no independent faculties. All its powers and forces are organically related like branches and leaves to a tree. For sound mental growth of the child Froebel suggests that there should be no gulf between home and school. The influence of the two should be organically connected, otherwise purpose of education is sure to be defeated.

Froebel contends that the unity between the various stages of mental growth — infancy, childhood, youth, manhood should not be lost sight of, otherwise education would be of no avail. There should be a connection between the various activities of the mind and the various aspects of life. Froebel calls this relation between the two 'inter-connectedness'. The realisation, of this inter-connectedness should constitute one great aim of education.

FROEBEL AND HERBART

Froebel directed the attention of the educators to the inner tendencies and impulses of the child. Herbart thought that a pupil may be made interested in a topic if it was connected with the already existing ideas in his mind leaving the circle of thought incomplete. Froebel stood for stimulating a spontaneous activity in order to create interest. Evidently, Froebel's conception is more sound and complete.

Herbart propounded the theory of correlation of studies. Froebel, too, wanted to establish an organic connection between the various studies. To Froebel knowledge was one organic whole like the tree and the various subjects of study were its branches like the shoots which spring from a single tree.

Herbart believed that mind consisted of presentations, but Froebel maintained that mind evolves from within.

Herbart could not explain what he exactly meant by an incomplete circle of thought. But Froebel's conception is quite clear. Once we excite an inherent tendency into action we are sure of a sustained interest. The theory of appealing to the natural impulses is perhaps the greatest achievement of Froebel. It is this theory that is gaining strength every day. Today educationists are realising more and more that the inborn tendencies of the child are of greatest importance in his education.

Froebel contradicts Herbart's theory that the new idea should be connected with the old. He maintains that instruction should aim at connecting the new interest with the old interests. If fresh interests are based on the innate impulses of the child they would be very easily acquired by him. Herbart attributes everything to experience. Froebel speaks of certain inborn tendencies and requires the educator to exploit the interests brought about by those tendencies. This training should harmonise with the innate tendencies of the child. The child's development is to be furthered not by means of dead imitation, but by spontaneous self-activity.

FROEBEL AND PESTALOZZI

From the very beginning, Froebel was keen to carry on the work which Pestalozzi had begun. A need was felt to deduce some educational principles from Pestalozzi's experience. Pestalozzi himself did not succeed in it. "Froebel, the pupil of Pestalozzi, and a genius like his master, completed the reformer's system; taking the results at which Pestalozzi had arrived through the necessities of his position. Froebel developed the ideas involved in them, not by further experience but by education from the nature of man, and thus he attained to the conception of true human development and to the requirements of true education" (Schmidt's Gesh, d. pad).

Froebel and Pestalozzi tried to do for the child what Bacon (1561-1626) did for philosophers nearly 200 years ago. Bacon advised the philosophers to use their own power of observation, to study nature, and not to depend upon what others have stated. Froebel and Pestalozzi likewise propounded the theory of self-activity for the child. But Pestalozzi only depended upon his theory of Anschaunng and had no other philosophical or psychological foundation. Froebel had clear notions about the innate tendencies and their organic development. Pestalozzi appears to be more of an educator than a philosopher. Froebel appears to be, on the other hand, a philosopher first and an educator afterwards.

THE CHILD'S OWN INDIVIDUALITY : SELF-REALISATION

The same divine principles work in every individual in a different manner. The child is not a blind follower. He does not accept everything told to him. He does only that which is related some how or other with his own way of doing things. To an observer he may appear to be imitating but in reality he does what suits his purpose in relation with his interests and impulses.

No two children develop in like manner even if they are kept in the same environment. Each child grows in his own way. Self-realisation may be described as an individual's development of natural inclination towards right direction. It is through the self-activity that a man can realise himself. Hence, neither a teacher nor an artificial atmosphere can be regarded as the sure means to arouse self-activity in the child. As a matter of fact, it must be determined by the child's own natural tendencies to action, only then it can produce some permanent effect. Active participation by the child is very important in the process of his self-realisation.

SELF-ACTIVITY IS CREATIVE

The result of education consists in what the child gives out from within himself. It does not consist in what the child learns from outside. Each child has a tendency to make new forms and combinations which suggest the new ideas and images arising in him. The child produces something which may appear to the adult as absurd and meaningless. But the divine principle is active also in the child as in the adult. So, whatever he produces must have some meaning or other. Thus, Froebel concludes that the development of self-activity is essentially creative. He devoted special attention to this attribute of creativeness in the child.

SCHOOL AN INSTRUMENT OF PROGRESS

Man is a social being. He is dependent on the people among whom he lives. This suggests the value of home, school, brotherhood and society. We so things being influenced by others. The individual and race make one great organic life. Froebel regards, the home, the school and the other institutions higher unities. The school is a place where the child learns in what way he is related with society in general. Thus, school is an instrument for the progress of the individual as well as of the society.

THE FUNCTION OF EDUCATION

To Froebel education is a stage in the evolution of the child. Education helps him to elevate him to a higher level and be a useful member of the society. By education he understands that he is a part of nature. Through education he becomes conscious of his unique existence and begins to seek his own place in the human society. He becomes ambitious to play his own part in the interactions of the society. Instruction should not be arbitrary. It should not aim at making the child mind a store of informations which he can utilise for his immediate purpose. It should always be slow, continuous and gradual in leading the child from the simple to complex, from the concrete to the abstract. The informations to be imparted to the child should be so natural and suitable to the present requirements of the child that he goes to school as if he is going to the playground.

THE KINDERGARTEN

Because of his theory of harmonious development Froebe attached very great importance to the earliest years o the child's life. He draws an analogy between the chil and the plant. Leaves and branches spring out of th tree according to the principle hidden in the seed Similarly, the child develops spontaneously by virtue o the tendencies and impulses he is born with. Froebe found his ideas of kindergarten — garden of children – from this resemblance between the growing child and th growing plant.

Self-Activity ; The Kindergarten

Froebel believed that full freedom should be given to th play of innate impulses of the child so that he may attai his maximum growth ultimately. This was the princip underlying his kindergarten system. The teacher shoul be able to understand the innate interests and tendencie of the child in order to perform his task successfully. H should promote self-activity in the children. All knowledg to be imparted to the children must appear to be comin out from their self-activities. Thus, knowledge will b regarded only as a means to an end, and the end i nothing but the growth of the self. The child must b given opportunities to get the habit of self-dependence i all the work of the school. The child in the school mus have the satisfaction that he has done something. In th process of doing something concretely he will expres himself and will lay bare his inner-self. Hence he mus learn by doing.

The Childhood is a Period of Play

The childhood is a period of play and not of work. "Th play is", says Froebel, "the highest phase of chil development — of human development at this period; fc it is self-active representation of the inner, representatio of the inner from inner necessity and impulse. Play is th purest, most spiritual activity of man at this stage..... It gives, therefore, joy, freedom, contentment, inner and outer rest, peace with the world. It holds the source of all that is good".[7]

If play is to have any educative value it should not be a purposive activity. But the play needs to be organised and controlled on definite materials in order to harmonise the feelings and the activities of the children while engaged in the activities. "Without rational conscious guidance", Froebel is reported to have said, "Childish activity degenerates into aimless play instead of preparing for those tasks of life for which it is destined".[8]

A New Method of Teaching

Song, Gestures and Construction

According to Froebel the child expresses his feelings and ideals through singing, gestures and constructing objects. On this belief he demanded that everything to be taught to the child must be expressed to him through singing, gestures and construction. This is a unique device which Froebel most remarkably invented. He recommended that history should be taught through dramatization or in a song. Froebel meant to stimulate the child's imagination and thought by placing concrete things before him.

The teacher should be very careful in the selection of songs, games and pictures because the child feels very much amused by them and tries to express himself while he is in their association. Froebel did not regard song, gestures and construction as isolated means to educate the child. He thought of them as three co-ordinate forms of expressions in the child. He saw an organic relation between them.

Gifts and Occupations

Gifts and occupations are the other means which Froebel used in the Kindergarten system. The gifts suggest to the child some form of activity. They are arranged in an order to be determined by the principle of development.

Occupations are the activities suggested by the gifts. The very order and arrangement of the gifts lead the child from the activities and thoughts of one state to those of another.

The First Gift : The first gift consists of a box of six woolen balls of different colours. The child is to roll them about in play. Rolling is the occupation. These woolen balls are meant to give to the child an idea of colour, particular stuff, form, motion and direction.

The Second Gift : In the second gifts there are a cube, a sphere and a cylinder of hard wood. In occupation with these things the child marks the difference, between the movements of the different articles. He sees that the cube is stable and the sphere is instable. He also notices that the cylinder is stable in certain positions and instable in others. Thus, the cylinder is noticed as possessing the quality of both the cube and the sphere. It is a concrete example of harmony of two opposite things in one.

The Third Gift : In the third gift there is a large wooden cube divided into eight equal parts. These cubes are meant to make the children understand the relation of parts with the whole. From these cubes the child may make a number of objects such as, chairs, tables, benches and stairs, etc.

In the other gifts come sticks, tablets and rings. While playing with these gifts the child gets the ideas of lines, surface and their inter-connections. The child has to engage himself in making a number of constructions with papers, sand, clay, wood and other materials.

The Teacher not Passive

In the Kindergarten, one should not think that the teacher is to remain entirely passive. As a matter of fact his responsibility is not lessened in any way. While the children are offered gifts, the teacher has to suggest the occupations connected with them. He has to demonstrate certain activities to them. When the teacher presents the gifts he sings a song connected with them and thereby tries to help the child to form appropriate ideas.

Play and Work

It is very significant to note that Froebel has not overlooked the growth of latter stages. To him as the play is the chief activity of childhood, similarly, work is the characteristic activity of boyhood. According to Froebel play and work are two of the essential stages in the process of the self-relation of the child. "Man works" he remarks, "that his spiritual divine essence may assume outward form, and that thus he may be enabled to recognise his own spiritual, divine nature and the inner-most being of God".[9]

The Curriculum

Froebel pays due attention to other subjects of the school curriculum. He divides the school curriculum in four parts, *viz.*, (1) Religion and religious instructions, (2) Natural science and mathematics, (3) Language, (4) Art and objects of arts. The school does not aim at "making each pupil an artist in some one or all of the arts, but to secure to each human being full and all-sided development".[10]

Discipline

Froebel believed in the theory of use and thought that various kinds of good traits may be developed in the child if his innate impulses are directed towards right direction. If we think only of the good our evil tendencies will disappear. Froebel was alive to the importance of self-control. To him, it is an inner discipline which is the cause of the outer discipline. If there is inner discipline the evil tendencies will never work and there will be no need of punishment.

IS FROEBEL CONSISTENT AND COHERENT ?

Inconsistency and incoherence mark the ideologies forwarded by Froebel. It is by gradual differentiation and modification of structured that development proceeds. Its continuity will be broken by the law of opposites which Froebel speaks of. The organic development does not take place by alteration from one extreme to another. All knowledge cannot come from within as Froebel conceived. Rationalism, too, in philosophy, accepted this method but proved a total failure because it could not cope with experience. "Internal development is stimulated by the external and modified by it; and process of making the internal external and the external internal are not as assumed by Froebel, successive but contemporaneous".[11]

Froebel is not very logical in the arrangement of verses. His pictures to be used in the method of teaching are rough and poorly drawn. He gives undue importance to his principle of organic unity. He tries to see it even where it cannot be detected. It is extremely difficult to understand the full significance of his symbolism. His symbols do not give us clear-cut notions of things they stand for.

CRITICISM OF FROEBEL'S THEORY AND PRACTICE

Froebel was bitterly critisised by many educational leaders even in his own time; and even today many are not in complete agreement with him. During his life time Prussia, the leading state in Germany, banned the establishment of Kindergartens. Froebel's socialistic and liberalizing tendencies were not liked by government authorities during his days.

The following have been the brief criticisms of Froebel raised by some educators :

(1) Froebel's excessive emphasis on play in education cannot be acceptable because it detracts the child from serious learning.

(2) Froebel's insistence upon play, constructive work, and many other subjects has under-rated the importance of true knowledge and leads to a disrespect for learning.

(3) As a philosopher, Froebel is discredited as a mystic and pantheist.

(4) Some criticise Kindergarten methods because of over-emphasis on form and mathematical knowledge due to Froebel's devotion to drawing and cubic building blocks.

(5) Many critics hold that Froebel's law of evolution does not explain definitely how to proceed in the development of child life.

THE SPIRIT OF FROEBEL'S THEORY ABOVE CRITICISM

Inspite of the above criticisms, no educational theory has been more followed in actual practice than that of Froebel. Froebel's educational principles have been accepted as basic for education at all levels — from the primary stage to the university. If we forget Froebel's eccentricities, his theory is compatible with the modern genetic psychology, sociology and industrial progress. Modern education will ever remain indebted to Froebel. All the best tendencies in modern education may be traced back to what Froebel stood for a century and a half ago. He is reported to have said that it would take a century for the universal acceptance of his views. We may not agree with many educational procedures propounded by Froebel, but it was he who first drew the attention of the society towards the education of very young children. "The formalism of the Kindergarten system may be subject to many criticisms. But its methodical arrangement of plays and occupations invited the active interest of many who lack the spirit of the master to give 'play' a place into schools".[12]

We admit that the songs and pictures used by Froebel are crude and rough, but he never meant that they should not be improved upon. He gave direction to the teacher to modify songs and pictures to suit the needs of the time. The underlying principles of Froebel's philosophy may not be intelligible at times, but his doctrines are of practical use. Just as Jesuits and Comenius introduced a systematic methodology of instruction, similarly Froebel gave a methodology of play to be applied in educational procedure.

Educational ideologies of Froebel were deeply coloured by the philosophy and scientific principles of his time. The essence of his contribution to education may be put in the words: 'self-activity' and 'creativeness'. The meaning of these words is being understood more and more as times pass on. Froebel stood for the recognition of the child's individuality in the school. Now the school is being regraded as a place where the teacher should try to discover the individuality of the child and devise means to develop the same. Activities, such as, play, songs, and constructing objects, etc., have been given an importance in the learning process of the child. Needless to say that all these tendencies in modern education may be traced back to Froebel's fundamental doctrines.

FROEBEL'S PERMANENT CONTRIBUTION TO EDUCATION

Froebel's permanent contributions to education may be summarised in the following way :

(1) The natural course of the evolution of the child's activities should be the main guide in education of the child.
(2) Inner self-activity directs the development.
(3) Early education should be organized around play.
(4) Physical, mental and moral powers should be developed and harmonized through constructive activity.
(5) Spontaneity and social control may be harmonized through creative activity.
(6) The curriculum should be based on the activities and interests of children.
(7) The education of women should be regarded as essential for the development of human race.
(8) Education can insure the future evolution of mankind.

SUMMARY

His Life

Developed a deep and abiding attachment to nature at a very tender and premature age. Deprived of parental affection. Moody, subjective and introspective by nature.

Turned towards the phenomena of nature companionship. Developed an intense sympathy for children.

Froebel learnt the principle and method of Pestalozzi and realized their inadequacies. He decided to devote his full life to the reform of free school training.

Only a few could understand him. Not appreciated in his own country, Germany. He thought that the U. S. A. would give full expression to his ideas.

Froebel's Faith in Spontaneous Growth

For the first time applied the idea of unity and spontaneous growth to education. Endeavours to see a unity in all things. Sees a continuity in the universe. Everything develops from within according to its own laws.

Froebel agreed with Leibnitz's theory of organic growth.

Theory of Inner Growth and Education

Froebel is wrong in thinking that all can be attained through development from within. An individual victim to the vicissitudes of life. Education needed to check deviation from the right path.

Froebel on Mental Development

Mental growth organic. Knowing, feeling and willing are the three major activities of the mind. Hence, any mental exercise must be in complete accord with these three activities.

Ascertain the divine message before giving any education.

Mind as a purposeful activity. Mind is a unity for sound mental growth. No gulf between home and school.

There should be a connection between the various activities of mind. Inter-connectedness.

Froebel and Herbart

Froebel stood for stimulating a spontaneous activity in

order to create interest. Herbart wanted to connect the new idea with the old for creating a interest.

To Froebel knowledge as an organic whole. Herbart for correlation of studies.

To Forebel mind evolves from within. To Herbart it consists of presentations. The theory of appealing to the natural impulses Froebel's greatest contribution.

Froebel for connecting the new interest with the old one. Herbart emphasises experiences. Froebel emphasises tendencies.

Froebel and Pestalozzi

Forebel completed Pestalozzi's work in a different way. Pestalozzi depended upon his theory of Anschaunng, and Froebel on innate tendencies and organic development. Pestalozzi was an educator first; and Froebel was a philosopher first.

The Child's own Individuality : Self Realisation

Each child has his own individuality.

Self-realisation is the development of nature inclination towards right direction.

Self-activity is creative.

School an instrument of progress.

The Function of Education

Education is to elevate the child to a higher level without making him directly conscious.

The Kindergarten

From an analogy between the child and the plant.

Self-activity : The Kindergarten

Full freedom to the play of innate impulses of the child—the principle of Kindergarten. The knowledge as a means.

The end is the growth of the self. The child to learn by doing.

The Childhood a Period of Play : Play should be rationally and consciously guided — but it should not be a purposive activity.

A New Method of Teaching : Songs, gestures and construction the chief means for stimulating the child's imagination.

Gifts and occupations to be selected and arranged according to the principle of child development.

The teacher is to suggest the occupations.

Play and work are the two different stages in the process of self-realisation.

The aim of education should be all-round development of the child. The curriculum accordingly.

Through disuse evil tendencies will die out. Ample opportunities for the practice of virtues needed.

Is Froebel Consistent and Coherent ?

Incoherence and inconsistency in Froebel's philosophy. Knowledge cannot be attained by mere evolution. Froebel carries his doctrine of organic unity too far. His symbolism fantastic.

Criticism of Froebel's Theory and Practice

Over emphasises play. Leads to disrespect for learning. A mystic and pantheist. Over-emphasis on form and mathematical knowledge. His law of evolution is not very clear.

The Spirit of Froebel above Criticism

All the tendencies in modern education find root in Froebel's conceptions. He made the society conscious of education for very young children. Gave a methodology of play. 'Self-activity' and 'creativeness' are becoming very popular in the modern educational procedures.

References

1. *Education of Man*. Hailmann's Trans., p. 162.
2. *Ibid.*
3. *Education of Man*, Hailmann's Trans. p. 5.
4. H.C. Browen on *Education of Man*.
5. Carlyle.
6. *Education of Man*, p. 13
7. Rusk : *Doctrine of Great Educators*, Chap. XI, p. 238.
8. Reminiscences, pp. 67-8.
9. *Education of Man*, 23.
10. *Ibid*, 85.
11. Rusk: *Doctrines of Great Educators*, Chap. IX, p. 260.
12. Cf. *Pedagogies of the Kindergarten*, pp. 233-4.

10

HERBERT SPENCER

(1820 — 1903)

His Life

Herbert Spencer was born in the county of Derby in England in 1820. His father was a school teacher, and a man of independent views. He believed in self-education. So, he encouraged Herbert to find out answers to his own problems. He did not like that Herbert should get involved in learning formal subjects of the school and thus lose his own independent way of thinking and arriving at the solution of problems. His father taught him physics, chemistry and geometry. So, he received a knowledge of these sciences early in life. His uncle taught him some school subjects, and at the age of seventeen he had the knowledge of an average school student.

About the year 1838 Herbert Spencer become interested in machines and thought to become a civil engineer. Afterwards, he decided to make a living by his own inventions. He could not succeed in the commercial line and turned to literature. In 1848, he became a sub-editor of The Economist, and in this capacity he came into contact with George Eliot, Huxley and Tyndall.

In 1858, Herbert Spencer left the sub-editorship of The Economist and relied for his living on independent writing alone. In 1855, he published The Principles of Psychology. From 1858 he began to issue A System of Philosophy in quarterly instalments. After this he began to publish books after books. Some of his principal writings are the following:

(1) Education, 1861.
(2) First Principles, 1862.
(3) The Principles of Biology, 1864-67.
(4) The Principles of Ethics, 1892-93.
(5) The Principles of Sociology, 1876-96.
(6) Essays, 1857-74.
(7) Various Fragments, 1897.
(8) Facts and Comments, 1902.
(9) Auto-biography, 1904.

Herbert Spencer was so much engrossed in his writings that he could not make a wide circle of friends. He lived mainly in Boarding Houses. In 1896, he went to reside at Brighton, where he died in 1903.

THE AIM OF EDUCATION

Spencer never loved old traditions. He wants to lead the child to a very high ideal by developing his interests. The child is to be made such that he may stand on his own legs by education himself. Spencer criticises the curriculum of his day because it lacked practical utility. In the educational system of his times adequate attention was not paid to the future preparation of children. According to Spencer the aim of education is to enable man to lead a complete and successful life. "To prepare us for complete living is the function which education has to discharge, and the only rational mode of judging of any educational course is to judge in what degree it discharges such a function".[1] In order to lead a complete life one must know how to develop his body and mind. He must know how to manage his whole affair, *i.e.* to bring up a family, to behave like a good citizen, to utilize all the means of comforts which nature has given, to use one's whole capacity for his own and social welfare. There are many sciences which throw light on these problems. Therefore, these sciences must be taught.

FIVE DIVISIONS OF MAN'S FUNCTIONS : EDUCATION

Spencer makes five divisions of man's functions in life. They are as follows :

(1) For self-preservation.
(2) For indirect self-preservation.
(3) For rearing of off spring.
(4) For social and political life in order to be an intelligent citizen and neighbour.
(5) For leisure of life.

Spencer thinks that man can fulfil all his above functions successfully if he studies the various sciences. We shall see below the kinds of sciences or the knowledge that, according to Spencer, one should try to study or acquire in order to be successful in the above five functions.

(1) *Self-preservation*

Nature takes care of all those things which are necessary for our self-preservation. But nature can look after self-preservation if we do not place any obstruction in our spontaneous activities. For picking- up the art of self-preservation, Spencer recommends the study of the sciences of physiology, hygiene, physics and chemistry. Spencer believes that a knowledge of these subjects will help one to preserve his health by furthering the various spontaneous activities.

(2) *Indirect Self-preservation*

Activities pertaining to indirect self-preservation are those which help one to make a successful living. Spencer can think of no such activities which do not require the help of sciences. We require the help of mathematics in various activities pertaining to our daily life. The various things we use every day, *e.g.*, food, clothings and house, are available to us through some kind of sciences. Geology, mathematics, chemistry, physics and astrology help us in many such vital activities. Spencer recommends the teaching of these sciences, because they prepare us for life.

(3) *Rearing of Offspring*

Spencer wants to give the knowledge of rearing of offspring to children in the school. The parents are generally ignorant of this knowledge. Hence, it is difficult for them to rear their children properly. Therefore, parents should be prepared for bringing up children.

(4) *Citizenship*

Spencer desires that the child should be a worthy citizen. He considers history very valuable in imparting the act of citizenship to children. But he criticises the history books of his times, because to him they are not written scientifically. So, he wants them to be re-written. To him, science is also a key to history. He thinks that history cannot be used properly without the knowledge of science. He has shown how history books should be written and how the various happenings should be described.

(5) *Leisure of Life*

Spencer has a very liberal outlook of life. So, he is fully alive to the necessity of education for utilizing leisure hour. For this he wants to teach painting, music, sculpture, literature and poetry to the child. But for the study of these arts, Spencer thinks that the child must study the science first, because the various sciences are at the root of all these fine arts. The fine arts may be made finer with the help of sciences. For example, a sculptor can make his art more living if he has a knowledge of anatomy and mechanics. A poet will infuse more life in his art if he knows those sciences which deal with the various pathological conditions. Needless to say that Spencer has failed to enter into the heart of fine arts. He wants to make every thing dependent on sciences. He could not understand the educative value of fine arts.

PRINCIPLES OF EDUCATION

Herbert Spencer has given us some very important principles of education. He is not very original in these principles. In fact, he has squeezed out the essence of the principles of education advocated by his predecessors and has given them to us in the form of maxims of education. However, these maxims are nearly universally adopted by educators in modern times.

From Simple to the Complex

The first of the principles advocated by Spencer is that "proceed from the simple to the complex". This principle means that first of all, simple things should be taught to children, because it is only after understanding these that they can follow difficult or complex ones. This maxim should be followed both in the organization and teaching of materials. If this maxim is not followed the children will feel no interest in what they are taught.

From Known to Unknown

Proceed from known to unknown is the second maxim of Spencer. New ideas are formed with the help of the old ones. In fact, the new ideas are a further continuation of the old ones. A child cannot understand a new idea unless he sees its relation to the already existing ideas in his mind. Therefore, while teaching, the teacher must decide how to connect the new ideas with the old ones. If the child realises that the new ideas are only a part of the ideas already in his mind, he will accept the new ideas very readily because they will be easily intelligible to him. Therefore, the teacher must begin with the known, *i.e.*, the ideas already known to the child, then he should proceed to show how the new ideas hitherto unknown are related with the known, *i.e.*, a further combination of the old ones. This maxim is so true that every teacher follows it even unknowingly.

From Indefinite to Definite

Proceed from indefinite to definite is the third maxim of

Spencer. Children's ideas are indefinite at first. As they grow, their ideas are clarified more and more. Therefore, it is quite natural to proceed from indefinite. Children know that these are stars, moon and the sun. But when they are given more knowledge about these, their notions become clarified further. Really speaking this does not appear to be a maxim of teaching. This is a psychological truth on which any principle of teaching might be based.

From Concrete to Abstract

Proceed from concrete to abstract is the fourth maxim of Spencer. First of all, the teacher should try to explain a thing through examples, then he may point to the generalization. For example, in teaching geometry, the students should be encouraged to make various kinds of forms. Then, with the help of these forms they may be taught some geometrical figures very easily.

Knowledge in Child through the Same Stages as in the Race

Another maxim of Spencer is that knowledge grows in the child through the same stages as it has passed through the race. Spencer believes that in the process of education the child should be made to pass all those stages through which the human race has passed in the process of its evolution. This is called the culture-epoch theory. The psychological basis on which this maxim is based is correct, but the inferences are unacceptable, because its propounders go too far. The propounders of the culture-epoch theory assert that the selection of matter and method of education should be made according to the stages through which the human race has passed. Spencer and his followers determined the method of education according to this theory, but they limited themselves to the life of children alone. They became indifferent to the full life responsibilities of man. Moreover, in the selection of matter we have to pay attention both to the child and the society. The society of today is different from what it was in the beginning of human civilization. The development of human civilization has followed a zigzag course. It will never be wise to follow this zigzag course. We will be obliged to drop out some of the courses. In fact, the education of the child should be determined in terms of his stages of development.

From Empirical to Rational

From the culture-epoch theory, Spencer infers another maxim of education that every subject should have an experimental introduction. In other words, Spencer advises to proceed from empirical to rational knowledge. There can be no objection to the maxim that every subject should have an experimental approach. However, it may be mentioned that this maxim is especially applicable to the teaching of science.

Tell Little and Lead to Infer much

Spencer holds that children should be told little and led to infer much. It is not easy to apply this principle, but its truth is accepted by all the educationists in the world. Spencer, himself was brought upon this principle. It is good if the children are to infer generalizations themselves. Thereby, they will be able to stand on their own legs. But this principle should not be taken to an unpredictable extent.

The Interesting Process of Education

Spencer's another maxim of education is that the process of education should be interesting and pleasurable to the child. There can be no objection to this principle. The process of education will be interesting to the child if all the natural tendencies of the child are exploited in his education. The education material should be so presented that they touch some of the natural dispositions of the child. If it is done, the child will feel interest and pleasure in learning a thing. Children take great interest and pleasure in observing, inquiring into and inferring from subjects which are connected some how or other with their natural dispositions.

SPENCER ON MORAL EDUCATION

Spencer criticises the general behaviour of parents towards children. He holds that the parents are generally unphysiological in their behaviour with children. They announce a rule of conduct, but care little to follow the same. In order to improve the society, Spencer likes to introduce certain reforms in the family itself. The children will be automatically improved if the parents and elders in the society try to place good examples before children. Spencer believes in Rousseau's principle of discipline by natural consequences. The parents should follow nature in determination of rules for giving punishment to children. Just as nature does not excuse any one against its laws, that is, if one puts his fingers in fire, the fingers are sure to be burnt, similarly if the parents decide about a rule of conduct, they must follow the same.

Spencer does not like unnatural punishment. He is in favour of giving natural punishment to children, whether the fault is minor or major. For example, if the child loses the knife of the kitchen, another knife should be bought by making a cut from his pocket money. If he disturbs the well-arranged things in a room, he should be made to re-arrange the same properly. If he spoils the walls, he should be required to wash the same. This is what Spencer means by natural punishment, and he is very right.

Spencer is of the opinion that children should not be treated harshly. Elders should treat them friendly. Children should be encouraged to acquire self-control and to manage their affairs themselves as far as possible.

Spencer's views on moral education, except his idea of discipline by natural consequences, are accepted to a great extent even today. It may be remarked here that there should be a limit to discipline by natural consequences. It is difficult to allow the child to suffer the natural consequences of his acts and learn. If we do so, the consequences might be fatal, and the child may hurt himself fatally. So, we shall have to keep a vigilant eye over his activities, or to arrange his atmosphere in such a way as to make it only educative.

SPENCER ON PHYSICAL EDUCATION

Spencer wants to base physical education of children on scientific principles. He says that children must not be scolded at the time of meals. There should be variety in the food. The clothes for summer should differ from those of winter. Specific place should be given to physical education in the school curriculum. Spencer points to the four existing defects in the modern physical education system : (1) Children are under-fed, (2) they are under-clothed, (3) adequate physical exercises are not given to them, and (4) they are made to do too much mental labour. Spencer has rendered a great service by making us conscious of the need of physical education of children, because success in life depends, both in physical and mental development.

AN EVALUATION OF SPENCER

Spencer's principles of education, intellectual, moral and physical have influenced greatly the theory and practice of modern education. His basis ideas are reflected in most of the practices and theories of education today. He has explained to us the great importance of science in the school curriculum. He has rightly pleaded for the freedom of the child in education.

Spencer is frequently criticised for the utilitarian character of his views, because he attaches little importance to the higher and sublime pleasures of life. By emphasising the utilitarian character of education, Spencer only meant "to gain for the neglected many what hitherto had been the prerequisite of the privileged few".

Spencer has emphasized the cultural elements in an entirely new way. He holds that all the phases of knowledge should be encouraged in any scheme of education so that every individual may have some attainment in each field. He was very democratic in this respect. He demanded a readjustment of education in such a way as to enable every individual to have that education which may equip him with all those tools which are necessary for a complete and happy living.

Spencer is also criticised on the point that he regarded education as a preparation of life and did not regard education as life itself. It is true that in his view that education should be a preparation of life. Spencer over-estimated the value of knowledge as a preparation. But this is characteristic of all those educators who advocated for a due place of sciences in the school curriculum. Moreover, it must be recognized that Spencer's position is but a reaction against the over-emphasis on method as advocated by the followers of the disciplinary conception of education.

As regards the question of method Spencer does not give us anything new. He has only elaborated a number of Pestalozzi's principles *e.g.*, education should proceed from the concrete to the abstract, and from simple to the complex, and so on. In his principle of moral education Spencer has followed only Rousseau, when he speaks of discipline by natural consequences.

Spencer's over-emphasis on the study of sciences by children in the school has been frequently criticised. But it must be noted that Spencer takes a very comprehensive meaning of science. In his definition of the term 'science' are included all the social, moral and natural sciences. As regards the contents of education Spencer appears to be against Rousseau. In this respect, he is nearer to Bacon and Locke. Spencer was against the traditional curriculum and method of education. He wanted to bring the school nearer to the needs of the individual in daily life. He wanted to bring in sciences by driving away the classics—Greek and Latin. He regarded science as the best means for the development of all human powers. Evidently, Spencer, even having a scientific spirit, could not rise above traditions. He failed to appreciate the importance of language. He regarded memory as the means for acquiring language. We cannot agree with him here.

SUMMARY

His Life

Spencer encouraged a person to stand on his own legs from the very beginning and find out solutions of his problems. Very much engrossed in writing books and essays.

The Aim of Education : Spencer not a blind follower of traditions. To lead the child to a very high ideal. The child to educate himself. The aim of education to prepare man for complete living. One must know how to develop body and mind. The study of sciences very helpful.

Five Divisions of Man's Function Education : Self-preservation; the study of physiology, hygiene, physics and chemistry.

Indirect self-preservation—successful living—the study of geology, mathematics, chemistry, physics and astrology.

Rearing of offspring—children to be given its knowledge.

Citizenship—The study of history.

Leisure of life— A liberal outlook of life. Leisure to be utililzed—painting, music, sculpture and literature to be taught but these, too, have to have their bases in the study of various sciences.

Principles of Education

From Simple to Complex.
From Known to Unknown.
From Indefinite to Definite.
From Concrete to Abstract.
Education according to the culture-epoch theory.
From Empirical to Rational.
Tell little and lead to Infer much.
The Interesting Process of Education.

Spencer on Moral Education : Elders and parents to place good examples before children. Believes in discipline by natural consequences.

Spencer against un-natural punishment.

Children not to be treated harshly. Should be encouraged to acquire self-control.

Spencer on Physical Education : To be based on scientific principles. Children not to be scolded at meals. Variety in food. Clothings suitable according to the season. Specific place to physical education in curriculum.

An Evaluation of Spencer : Spencer's influence on modern education profound. Explained the importance of the curriculum. Advocated for freedom of the child.

Spencer is criticised for his utilitarianism. Failed to appreciate the sublime pleasures of life. But Spencer very democratic.

Stood for all the phases of knowledge for the individual. Stood for complete living for all.

Regarded education as a preparation for life and life itself. This is against the modern tendency in education.

Spencer follows Pestalozzi in his maxims and follows Rousseau in his conception of discipline.

Takes a very comprehensive view of science and includes social, moral and natural sciences. Spencer nearer to Bacon and Locke regarding the content of education. Against the traditional curriculum. Wanted to bring education nearer to the demands of the daily life of the individual. Drives away classics. Regarded science as the best means for the development of all human powers. Spencer could not rise above traditions. Failed to appreciate the importance of language.

References

1. Herbert Spencer — quoted in "*Brief Course in the History of Education*" by Monroe, Paul, p. 356, Macmillan, 1907.

11

MONTESSORI, MARIA

(1870 — 1952)

Her Life

Dr. Maria Montessori, an Italian citizen was born in 1870. During her early days Italy was undergoing great political upheavals. By coming into contact with feeble-minded children she realised that such children were more in need of education than of medical treatment. At a conference of teachers, she advocated her stand-point. Soon after she studied the methods of Lombroso and Sergi and established a school for feeble-minded children. By some experiment she discovered that the defective children trained by her did better than many normal children taught in other schools. This encouraged her to apply her new method in the teaching of normal children as well and she thought that her method would further the mental development of all children.

In order to make her method more adequate Montessori studied experimental psychology and social anthropology. As a superintendent of children's houses she worked harder on her new methods of teaching and demonstrated the adequacy and utility of the same. She asserted that her method was adequate enough to develop muscles, to give the much desired sense-training and inculcate the spirit of freedom in children.

MONTESSORI AND OTHER EDUCATORS

Rousseau wrote a new chapter in the history of education

by his introduction of naturalism in it. But he stretched his theory too far when he asserted that we should lose the child's time rather than gain it. He exposed the evil consequences of the old un-natural methods of teaching and stressed the need of studying the child.

Pestalozzi tried to psychologise education on his theory of Anschaunng, which is his chief contribution. Herbart's theories of apperception and of ideas are his main contribution to education. Forebel's educational doctrines are coloured with the German philosophy of the day. His ideas of 'organic unity' and 'spontaneous activity' and 'creativeness' are his chief contributions to the principles of education. Herbert Spencer showed the value of the study of sciences in schools and popularised some of the universally accepted maxims of education.

Montessori was deeply impressed by the natural trend of Rousseau and in all her work his influence is quite visible. Montessori did not suffer from any limitations of psychological nature like those of her predecessors because by her time psychology had grown into an independent branch of study. Experiments were being carried out in various branches of this science. Montessori was thoroughly familiar with these experiments and she knew what was being done in psychological laboratories in connection with mental activities of young children. Because of all these advantages, she naturally carried further the psychological movement forwarded by Pestalozzi. She says, "The broader the teacher's scientific culture and practice in experimental psychology, the sooner will come for her the marvel of unfolding life, and her interest in it".[1] Rousseau emphasised the need of studying the child, but there was no psychological data before him to recommend specific prescriptions to the teacher. Montessori, on the other hand, could recommend the methods of experimental psychology and practically showed that a teacher would proceed with his lesson better if he utilized the results of experimental psychology.

If we take out Froebel's symbolism and mystic philosophy he appears much like Montessori. It is difficult to understand what Froebel exactly means when he says that gifts have symbolic values. Similarly, one cannot easily understand the mystic value of 'occupation'. On the other hand, Montessori is very simple in her recommendations. She recommends ordinary things for children to play with. The children are asked to occupy themselves in the way in which ordinary human beings do. The games are to be so organized as to have educational value without any philosophical or symbolic significance. While engaged in playing the child is stimulated to acquire knowledge which he needs for some immediate purpose. The things with which the children are to play are called 'didactic materials' which is the most original part of the Montessori method.

THE PSYCHOLOGICAL MOMENT

The needs of the child differ at different times. The teacher must be able to understand them and all his efforts must be directed only towards their fulfilment. He is to give active help in the normal growth of the child. By 'psychological moment' in the educational process we should understand that moment at which the child is conscious of a need. Montessori says that it is the duty of the teacher to catch this moment. This is what the employment of psychological method in education should suggest to the teacher. The teacher is not to ignore any need of the child. Failure of the child in some of his work may be attributed to the absence of psychological moment, and the teacher must wait for it.

THE CHILD RESPONSIBLE FOR HIS DEVELOPMENT

Montessori says that the teacher should suggest to the child indirectly that the virtue in its own reward. The child is very happy when he accomplishes something. He takes immense of pleasure in his self-development. He feels very much proud at his success in some area of activity. This success is the greatest reward to him. Hence Montessori makes no provision for prizes in her system. She considers the development of virtue its own reward. She makes the child responsible for his own growth. She suggests that the external interference is to be lessened day-by-day with the gradual development of the child. Thus the child will automatically develop in himself, the virtues of initiative, self-reliance and power of concentration. The pupil must be taught to his own individuality. This must be made sacred to him. The child in the Montessori method is expected to acquire the habits of serious work and diligence rather than those of obedience and dependence.

THE MONTESSORI SYSTEM

Montessori makes the child free to develop according to his own nature. In a Montessori school children from three years of age to seven years are found totally engrossed in their work. Some are engaged with exercises on senses, others with arithmetic exercises, and others playing with balls etc. Some are found seated on a table and some on the carpet of the floor. Children are often found shouting at their victories, such as "Teacher! teacher! see what I have done". There is an atmosphere of freedom in a Montessori school. Hence discipline becomes self-controlled and it presents no problem, except sometimes in individual cases which are handled by isolation. Every child has a regard for other's claims. Hence there prevails a feeling of friendliness and goodwill.

The child in a Montessori school is made free to engage himself in various activities which are organised deliberately within educative surroundings. The child enjoy freedom, but there is no chaos in the school. Everywhere we find a routine. There is no chance for the child to be idle, because he is permitted to do whatever interests him. He may sit on the table or on the chair. The furniture is so light that he can move it any where he likes, 'Occupations' and games are such as to train the child into his daily duties such as dressing, undressing, washing and brushing etc.

Thus we see that a Montessori school is characterised by the principles of liberty, spontaneity and freedom. There is no rigid time-table to be followed. Punishments are discouraged and reward are not favoured. Under such circumstances discipline presents no problem. A Montessori school appears to be a regime of children's *Swaraj* (Self-government). This is the freedom which Rousseau advocated. Miss Parkhurst, too, in her Dalton Plan has favoured this freedom for the child. The pupil is a free agent in his education, free to select his subject, time and speed.

Sensory Training

The First Stage in Education

In her school first of all Montessori lays special stress on the training of senses of touch, sight and hearing when children are quite young. Various games and occupations are employed for this. Children are placed in circumstances where they know things, their names, and the ideas connected with them. By personal and practical experience the child is explained the difference between hot and cold. The same method is employed to let him know the distinction between high and low, round and oval, rough and smooth, and thick and thin etc. Montessori has selected her material purely from pedagogical point of view. Hence most of the materials chosen for training perception of size and form differ from the Froebelian gifts.

Differences between the Deficient and Moral Child

Montessori made little distinction for testing sensory activity and for sense education between normal and subnormal children. But she found three main differences between them : (1) The subnormal children for sensory training required objects representing striking contrast to one another. Whereas the normal ones were satisfied with objects which had fine distinctions. (2) The feeble-minded children were satisfied with only one successful operation and had no pleasure in repeating their successful experiments. But the normal ones took interest in repeating their successful operations. (3) The deficient child lacks initiative in correcting his mistakes himself and craves very often for the help of the teacher, while the normal child takes pleasure in correcting himself. These observations lead Montessori to conclude that the Didactive Material necessary for educating the deficient child stimulates self-education in the normal one.

The Second Stage

In the second stage of education, while playing the children are to build tower by blocks, broad and long stairs and thus grasp the difference between length and breadth. They find objects scattering here and there and they are to distinguish between larger and smaller ones. The broad stair suggests to them the distinction between thickness and thinness. The long stair-exercise leads them to an appreciation of strength. To develop odour-sense they are to sort and grade sixty four cards of various coloured wools. Thus the children develop an association of the sensory perception with the name. They can recognise objects corresponding to their names and remember the names corresponding to the objects.

Montessori is of opinion that writing is easier than reading. In reading one has to understand certain signs and fine changes of voice. This is by no means an easy task for the child. By virtue of its nature writing is more mechanical than intellectual. Because of these reasons, Montessori favours teaching of writing first. The child is taught writing through games in which he uses raised letters of the alphabets. Thus, the child learns how to write without being conscious about it.

The Third Stage

At the third stage of education the child is trained to appreciate forms. The child has to fit certain pieces into their corresponding holes. Training of senses of slight, touch and muscles are further given. From solid objects the child is led to appreciate plane figures represented by mere lines and perceived only visually. Thus, he passes from the concrete to the abstract.

At this stage the child is given training in reading. By reading Montessori does not mean only producing of certain sounds on seeing certain signs on the paper. She considers it merely as 'barking at print'. She wants that the child must be able to understand what he reads.

The Fourth Stage

In the fourth stage the children are trained in practical duties of life, such as, how to put the furniture of the room in order and attend to minute details of personal cleanliness. In order to develop their muscles they are given certain rhythmic physical exercises. They are introduced to water-colours and free-arm drawing from nature. Lessons in reading, writing and arithmetic are given. They are encouraged to write composition comprising of only words and phrases. They play certain games with pebbles, poles and counters and learn counting thereby. The children have not to stand tiresome commands and instructions of the teacher. Under the influence of appropriate didactic materials everything goes in the most natural manner. The children learn reading, writing and arithmetic while playing with didactic materials. This feature of the process has aroused popular interest in the Montessori method.

THE PSYCHOLOGY OF TEACHING WRITING

Montessori applies a psychological method in the teaching of writing. To her the subject is more important than the object. The individual who writes is more important than the writing itself. She wants that the child should be trained first in some preparatory movements before he is actually trained in writing. These movements should be made mechanical by repeated exercise. After this the child may be made to write without being conscious of having learnt anything in the connection previously. All of a sudden an impulse is aroused in him and he begins to write and get immense pleasure in doing so. He feels that he has learnt some thing without being taught.

KEYS TO THE MONTESSORI METHOD

We hint below at the substance of the Montessori methods:

(1) To train the children individually independent of others.
(2) It is the senses to be appealed to rather than the intellect.
(3) Sense of touch is fundamental. It must not be neglected at the early stage, otherwise it will lose its susceptibility.
(4) The child is to be helped actively in his normal expansion.
(5) Exercise to be used should correspond to the need of development felt by an organism.
(6) Wait for the psychological moment. Do not teach anything until its need exists.
(7) No rigid time-table.
(8) No prizes. Self-development is the reward.
(9) Correction should come from the didactic material and not from the teacher.
(10) Auto-education of Rousseau and Spencer.
(11) Intellectual discipline by consequences.
(12) Perfect freedom to the child. Absolute obedience to laws of development of child's own nature.
(13) Liberty to the children in their spontaneous manifestations.

The Method of Montessori System

(a) The Exercises of Practical Life.
(b) The Exercises in Sensory Training.
(c) The Didactic Exercises.

(a) The Exercises of Practical Life

(1) Let the child learn to take care of nails, hands,

teeth, buttons, press, etc.

(2) Training in liberty.
(3) Things in the House of Childhood to be arranged in order without making noise.
(4) To make children accustomed to ascending and descending stairs, etc., etc.

(B) Sensory Training with Didactic Materials

(1) Isolate the senses whenever possible.
(2) Auditory exercises to be given in an environment not only of silence but even of darkness.
(3) Wooden cylinders, rods, and blocks of various sizes to be used in the training of the perception of size.
(4) Geometrical insets in metal for perception of form.
(5) Tablets of wood, etc., for discrimination in weight.
(6) For touch — highly polished surface and a sand paper surface.
(7) For sense of temperature — hot and cold water.
(8) For auditory acuity — cylindrical sound boxes containing different substances.
(9) For the colour-sense — graded series of coloured wood — 64 cards of various colours.
(10) The lesson to be divided into three steps,

   (a) The association of the sensory percept with the name.
   (b) Reading the name corresponding to the object.
   (c) The teaching of writing precedes teaching of reading etc., etc.

A CRITICISM OF MONTESSORI METHOD

Montessori does not appear to be sound in her theory that the child will derived pleasure from his mere capacity of sensory discrimination. Sensory training will be undoubtedly very useful in training of handling objects of daily use. But the training of senses for its own sake is questionable. It is difficult to believe that the ability to distinguish a large number of sensations would itself give any pleasure to anybody. But Montessori over emphasises this aspect of sensory training.

Montessori does not believe in literary training and in the training of imagination at early stages. She adheres to the theory that the development in the child corresponds to the development in the race. Therefore, every child should undergo the stages which the human race has passed through. The primitive man did not use any literature. His life was dominated by practical activities. Accordingly the child's early stages must be dominated by practical activities.

Montessori meant her houses of childhood for poorer children. Herein we find a justification for Montessori's exclusion of literary side of education. Children belonging to lower strata of society could not have actually appreciated literature. But if we want to extend the Montessori system for the benefit of all classes of children, it will be necessary to give a place to literary training as well.

Perhaps Montessori regards that imagination is not a part of child's life. To her imagination is opposed to the real and identical with the imaginary. The child is already full of phantasies, So there is no reason to develop them further. She does not like that the children should read fairy tales and myths etc., because they will make the children more phantastic. Montessori says, "In fact when we are told that a child 'no longer believes in fairy tales', we rejoice". We say then : "He is no longer a baby".[2] Montessori desires that the child should be given training in practical life from the earliest years, so that he may not be a dreamer. The child must be brought into contact with the objects of real world in order to make him successful in the practical tasks of life.

Elementary training is very good and it is desirable that the child should be brought into contact with real objects. Education does not aim at preparing dreamers. No undue stress should be given to develop the child's phantastic imagination, otherwise it may produce a pathological state of mind. But it is difficult to agree with Montessori in her scheme of developing the children altogether from myths and tales etc., wherein lies the seeds for the growth of the literary, dramatic of artistic mind. Drever very aptly remarks, "to repress the child in this respect is to cut him off from the language which Homer, Dante and Shakespeare speak, and to shut him out from the world of ideal and truth and beauty".[3]

What is true in the West regarding the world of Dante and Shakespeare is true in India about the world of Kalidas and Tagore etc. Culture would give a distorted appearance to the Indian child if he is cut off from the *Ramayana* and *Mahabharat* when his imagination-activity is at its height. For a harmonious integration of the mind it is necessary that it is susceptible to the great ideals of truth and beauty. The child must be introduced to indigenous stories. But the child should not be given scope for mental wanderings in the attempt at developing and training his aesthetic imagination. Conformity to a world of solid and definite fact is atleast as essential as the development of the ideal world."[4]

Montessori wants that the child should acquire the knowledge of the three R's very early. She prescribes very remarkable method for teaching of the three R's. But there are other things as well which the child needs learn before he learns these. Education should enable the child to understand things surrounding him. In the beginning the child does not require the knowledge of three R's. So it is desirable to postpone it for the later years when he desires it most.

Montessori stands for training the senses in isolation wherever possible. The Gestalt psychology has proved the invalidity of this notion. It is the perception of the whole, and not in parts, that gives us an idea of a particular object. Hence the training of senses in isolation is not sound psychologically.

SUMMARY

Her Life

Studied Lombroso and Sergi she founded a school for defective children. Applied her new method on normal children as well and uncouraged by its success. Her method for developing muscles, sense training, and freedom for children.

Montessori and other Educators

Montessori stands in sharp contrast to Rousseau, Pestalozzi, Herbart and Forebel because of the age she lived in.

Montessori carried forward Pestalozzi's psychological movement.

Goes further than Forebel. Does not indulge in symbolism and mysticism. Recommends children to play with ordinary children.

The Psychological Moment

The teacher to wait for it. He must understand the immediate need of the child and direct his efforts to fulfil the same.

The Child Responsible for his Development

No external influence to obstruct the natural activities of the child. The child to acquire the virtues of initiative, self-dependence and industry.

The Montessori System

Complete freedom to the child. Every one to play according to his own peculiar interest. No problem of discipline. The occupations with the Didactic Materials are determined by organized circumstances which lead to train children in their daily duties.

No timetable. No rigid course. School a regime of children's *Swaraj* (Self-government).

Sensory Training : The First Stage : Training of senses the first stage in education.

Three main differences between the deficient and normal child.

The Second Stage : Training of the eyes and writing. To distinguish between smaller and larger objects. To develop a colour sense. Writing to be taught before reading.

The Third Stage : To appreciate from concrete to abstract. Training in reading.

The Fourth Stage : Training in the duties of practical life. Rhythmic physical exercises. Use of water colours.

Free-arm drawing from nature. Lesson in arithmetic through games.

The Psychology of Teaching Writing : The writer more important than writing. Preparatory movements necessary in order to make the child write without being conscious of it.

A Criticism of Montessori Method

Pleasure to be derived from the capacity of sensory discrimination is a pre-supposition. No training of senses for its own sake.

Literary training and the training of imagination neglected. The child need not undergo all the stage through which the human race has passed. Literary training necessary.

To Montessori imagination not a part of child life. Child is already full of phantasies. No attempt to develop them further. The child to be made a dreamer, but practical.

The literary, dramatic and artistic senses to be developed in the child. Hence he is not to be cut off from tales altogether.

The knowledge of the three R's given too early at the cost of other necessary thing.

Training of senses in isolation is unpsychological.

References

1. Tozzier: *An Educational Wonder Worker*, p. 89.
2. *The Advanced Montessori Method*, p. 257.
3. Drever : *An Introduction to the Psychology of Education*, p. 199.
4. Drever : *op. cit.*, p. 199.

12

JOHN DEWEY

(1859 — 1952)

His Life

John Dewey is not only one of the greatest philosophical thinkers that the United State of America has produced, but he may be also placed amongst the world's greatest philosophers and educators. He has been universally accepted as a great humanist and a great educator. He has exercised a profound influence on the schools not only of America but also of other countries. His students have spread his fame as a philosophical thinker and educational reformer to foreign countries. He has been invited by several countries, like Japan, China and U.S.S.R. to lecture on various problems of education. Turkey and U.S.S.R. requested him to help them in the reorganization of their school systems. Since Pestalozzi no modern educational thinker has enjoyed so much universal honour and fame.

John Dewey was born in 1859 at Burlington, Vermont. He received his education mainly in the public schools of the town and at the University of Vermont. He received his Ph.D. degree from the John Hopkins University. At John Hopkins he studied philosophy under George S. Morris and Charles S. Pierce, political and institutional history under Herbert B. Adams and psychology under G. Stanley Hall.

Dewey was a teacher for some time in the University of Michigan. In 1894 he was appointed the head of the department of philosophy at the University of Chicago. At

Chicago he established the University Elementary School which exercised a remarkable influence on the educational theory and practice in America. In 1904 he was appointed a professor of philosophy in Colombia University, New York City. For nearly three decades he worked at this post.

Dewey's Chief Educational Writings. Dewey has produced a large number of books and hundreds of articles. Many of his publications are on pure philosophy. Below is given a list of his chief works on education :

1896 — Interest and Effort as Related to Will.
1899 — The School and Society.
1902 — The Child and the Curriculum.
1910 — How We Think?
1913 — Interest and Effort in Education.
1915 — Schools of Tomorrow (with Evelyn Dewey).
1916 — Democracy and Education.
1920 — Reconstruction in Philosophy.
1922 — Human Nature and Conduct : An Introduction to Social Psychology.
1925 — Experience and Nature.
1929 — The Quest for Certainty : A Study of the Relation of Knowledge and Action.
1929 — Sources of a Science of Education.

DEWEY'S PHILOSOPHY

In order to understand Dewey's principles of education, one must have an idea of his basic philosophy. For this onwards we shall briefly hint at Dewey's views on the nature of mind and knowledge.

Mind

Dewey believes in the evolution of mind and intelligence in a natural way. He thinks that these are the results of man's activities directed to solve the varied practical and social problems of life. Mental powers go on developing as they are employed in the ordinary activities of daily existence. Mind is a most effective instrument in helping man to solve his problems. It is because of this instrument that man has made himself superior to all other creatures on earth.

Mind, as an instrument, includes all its three aspects—thinking, feeling and willing. Dewey does not regard knowledge as apart from the mind. To him ideas are mere activities of the mind. Ideas are developed by the individual in the process of controlling the objects of the environment for avoiding pain or obtaining satisfaction. This is the instrumental theory of mind which Dewey has propounded.

Knowledge

Dewey does not believe that knowledge precedes action. It is only as a result of action that knowledge is inferred. Action comes before experience which is the source of knowledge. Just as a child after experience gets the knowledge that fire burns one's hand, similarly all his learning is based on experience. Experience, knowledge or learning is a by-product of action. People ordinarily believe that knowledge arises apart from action, and regard it as an independent existence. But Dewey will not agree with this point of view. He says that knowledge can never arise apart from action. It is always related some action somehow or other. Whatever significance or meaning a knowledge may possess, it is always related to what a person does not wants to do. Dewey holds that if knowledge is thus derived from action, it should not be departed from the activities responsible for its production. Knowledge can have no significant existence when it is dissociated from action.

Dewey believes that all knowledge has come as a result of activities of individuals in their struggle for existence. The struggle for shelter, food and colthing resulted in certain activities which ultimately formed certain tendencies as instincts, impulses, and interest which are inherited by us to-day. These inherited tendencies are not as fixed and definite in human individuals as they are in the animals. These tendencies are general urges which respond to the various stimulations present in the environment. It is through the play of these tendencies or general urges that human intelligence is developed. Therefore, Dewey thinks that the natural play of these tendencies should be considered as the starting point of the educational process of the child.

Dewey regards knowledge as a social instrument, that is, as a means of social progress. This standpoint is one of his chief contributions.

The Process of Thinking

In his book 'How We Think' Dewey explains the process of thinking. Dewey holds that thinking does not take place in a vacuum; *i.e.* pure contemplation cannot be its basis. Nor does it originate from mass of sensations. Thinking starts from some cause. It is only a cause which stimulates one to think. If the activity of the individual goes on smoothly, he has nothing to think about. But when his progress is obstructed, he is obliged to think. Hence it is a problem confronted by the individual which stimulates thinking. Thus Dewey explains how a problem stimulates thinking : "A question to be answered, an ambiguity to be resolved, sets us an end and holds the current of ideas to definite channel. Every suggested conclusion is tested by its reference to this regulating end, by its pertinence to the problem in hand".[1] To Dewey thinking is a function of activity. In the process of thinking one undergoes a series of experimentations in order to reach the needed solution of the problem.

Dewey mentions five logical steps in the process of thinking. They are as follows :

(1) The feeling of a doubt, hesitation, difficulty or a problem.
(2) Taking the whole situation in view of analysing its carious elements, and then locating the heat of the problem.
(3) Arising of suggestions and following the same to find out the possible solutions.

(4) The bearings of each solution are developed and subjecting the most possible solution to experimentation.
(5) To observe and experiment further in order to accept or reject the solution.

Dewey believes that every normal mind follows the above five steps in the solutions of any problem. Comenius has already hinted at these five steps indirectly. But the credit goes to Dewey for making the educators fully conscious of this process in the development of the mind. On this principle Dewey advocates that instruction to be given to the child should follow the normal course of mental activity. This principle is at the base of Project Method, Problem Method and the Activity Programme.

DEWEY'S PHILOSOPHY OF EDUCATION

What is Education ?

Dewey regards education an indispensable social progress. To him society cannot progress without the help of education. Education is a process by which civilization is preserved and is developed further. Dewey says that education is "the process of the reconstruction or reconstitution of experience, giving it a more socialized value through the medium of increased individual efficiency. The inner and outer experiences of the individual are always changing. The individual has to face new situations and problems from time to time. Hence his activities should also be changing accordingly. Thus experience is revised, reorganized or reconstructed. To Dewey this growing, changing, or revising of experience is education. Thus Dewey 'put the meaning of education within the process'. He does not believe that education starts only when the child begins to go to school. He thinks that education begins since the very birth of the child, and goes on throughout the whole life. Thus education is regarded as life itself, and not as a preparation for life.

The Aim of Education

Dewey does not believe in any ultimate aim of education. In his Democracy and Education[1] writing on education he says, "It has all the time an immediate end, and so far as activity is educative it reaches that end — the direct transformation of the quality of experience. Infancy, youth, adult life — all stand on the same educative level in the sense that what is really learned at any and every stage of experience constitutes the value of that experience...."[2] Thus Dewey finds the aim of education in the process itself. The aim of education is not to reach any prefixed final goal. In fact, the aim is the immediate and catching attention. Education is to remake experience. Hence it is always to move further towards new activities and revising of experience. As Dewey says, "The process of education is a continuous process of adjustment, having as its aim at every stage an added capacity of growth."[3] The individual has always to readjust himself in the environment. So long this process of readjustment is continued education goes on. Since this readjustment never stops and the individual is always in the process of learning things, education never stops in life. Evidently, no such final goal or end of education can be conceived at which education is to be completed. Furthermore, the aim of education is not to be determined by the teacher. It is the child himself who has to choose his own aim.

Education is Life Itself

Dewey emphasizes that education is life itself, and not a preparation for life. A remote aim of education can not be appealing to the child. It is only an immediate aim that can be interesting to him. The whole process of education becomes discouraging to the child if he is required to put in efforts for an aim which is not immediate pertaining to his felt need. The child lives in the present. The future is meaningless to him. Hence it is absurd to require him to do things for some future preparation. As the child lives in the present the process of education is identical with the process of the present life itself.

Dewey speaks of two fundamental factors in the educational process, the individual and the social. We shall understand these below :

The Individual Factor in Education

Dewey regards the child as the core of the whole educational process. He says, "education must begin with a psychological insight into the child's capacities, interests, and habits. . . .[4] These powers, interests, and habits must be continually interpreted — we must know what they mean. They must be translated into terms of their social equivalents — into terms of what they are capable of in the way of social service". Dewey looks at the child's capacities and interests in a social context, thinking that it is in the soical context alone that they can be developed. Dewey speaks of four instincts or fundamental interests of the child, *viz.*, (1) the interest in conversation, (2) the interest in inquiry or finding out things, (3) the interest in construction, (4) the interest in artistic expression".[5]

Dewey thinks that the child's interest in conversation is the greatest of all educational resources. But all these four interests may be accepted as the basis of the curriculum of the school, because these represent the great racial activities, such as communicating each other's thought, procuring food, obtaining shelter, and making clothing. Dewey believes that if education is conducted on these lines the child will develop into a healthy personality and will acquire such traits which will help him in reconstructing new experiences.

The Social Factor in Education

Dewey cannot conceive of an individual apart from the society. To him both the individual and the society exist at the same time. When we think of an individual, we can think about him only in some kind of social context. An individual can have no independent existence. He is born in a society, he grows in a society and lives in a society. He is able to develop his various powers by coming into contact with his fellows in society. It is only by living in a society that he becomes human and acquires the necessary modes of responses and conduct which make him an individual.

If the individual is dependent upon society, the society, too, is an organic union of individuals. The activities of the individual centre round social intercourse, relations, interactions. Dewey regards the family as the first social institution which awakens the powers of the child into activity. The child takes part in the home activities because he realises that they give satisfaction to him and to others. At birth the child's capabilities are undeveloped. They are developed as he begins to take increasingly greater interest in home and other social activities. In the beginning the activities of the child are self-centred. Therefore he must be helped to realise the ends and purposes of society. For this, it is necessary to organize the school for co-operative action. Thus, Dewey has emphasized the need of this reorganizing. This idea of socialization is Dewey's educational contribution of the highest importance.

THE SCHOOL

Dewey regards school as an institution essential to social life. To him school is an absolute social necessity. The school is not a place where some knowledge is imparted and an attempt is made to develop certain habits in children. To Dewey the school is a place where the child will learn by his own experiences. At the school the child will make many experiments in his life in order to learn how his life is directly dependent on the continued growth of the society. As a social institution the school will try to develop a social consciousness in the child so that he may be able to derive the maximum benefit from what the society has to offer him. The school should try to develop in the child powers which he can use for furthering the ends of the society as a whole.

The school is to be a representative of the society outside. Its activities should reflect the needs and problems of the society. These activities should try to inculcate in children the habits of co-operation and mutually useful living.

The school should grow out of the home life. There should be no sudden break in the activities of the child in the home and in the school. In the beginning the school should try to preserve, continue and rebuild those activities with which the child has been familiar in the home. Thus the school should provide to the child the atmosphere of the home in a retouched and more scientific form. In this school the children will carry on common programme of educative experiences.

In Dewey's school no formal moral lesson will be necessary. In fact, the pupils will receive moral education through social and combined activities. To Dewey entering into proper relation with others in a unity of work and thought is the best moral training, and he wants to organize the work of the school towards this ends as well.

The school should try to make the society conscious of its own needs by giving the people a clear conception of the needs and problems of the modern life. The school is also to formulate those ideals which will guide the fulfillment of these needs, but these ideals have to emerge from the life of community itself.

In his school Dewey gives an important place to the teacher. Dewey regards the teacher as a social servant. The teacher is not to impose his personality on the child. He has to guide the growth of the child in a social atmosphere. He should select those influences which are helpful in developing the right attitudes in children, and he has to see that the children respond and react to these influences properly.

THE CURRICULUM

We may infer from the above account that Dewey has no sympathy with the traditional curriculum. Dewey does not like the division of knowledge into particular branches.

He says that "We violate the child's nature and render difficult the best ethical results by introducing the child too abruptly to a number of special studies, of reading, writing, geography, etc."[6] To Dewey, it is the child's own activities around which the school subjects should be organized and not around science, literature, history or geography. It is with the 'activities' that the child has seen in the home that the school should begin its work, and not with the teaching of reading, writing and arithmetic. Dewey says, "The beginning is made with child's expressive activities in dealing with the fundamental social material, — housing (carpentry); clothing (sewing); food (cooking). These direct modes of expression......bring out...... the factors of social communication — speech, writing, reading, drawing, moulding etc."[7] Thus, the curriculum in primary school should be organized according to the fourfold interests of the child — in conversation, inquiry, construction and artistic expression.

According to Dewey the curriculum should consist of educative experiences and problems. The aim is to enrich the already gained experiences. The problems to be included in the curriculum should be so organized as to inspire the pupil to add to the existing knowledge and ideas. It should be noted that Dewey uses the words 'educative experiences' in a special sense. According to Dewey only those experiences are educative which pay due regard to the natural inclinations of the child in the context of the social, political, physical, economic and political conditions of the community. Thus in Dewey's curriculum, books, teachers and apparatuses will be subordinated to the felt interest of the child.

Dewey suggests that the curriculum must develop critical discrimination in the pupil so that the latter may develop the capacity to choose intelligently from the various alternatives facing him. This is possible only if the materials to be taught are taken from the day-to-day life. The context of each subject should link the present with the past, but at the same time the immediate usefulness of the context must emphasized. Moreover, different subjects should not be presented as the particular branches of study. They should be correlated and linked together in such a way as to give the impression that they are items of a single process by which the continuance and growth of the society is assured.

THE METHOD OF TEACHING

Dewey emphasizes direct experience as the basis of all method. To him knowledge should arise from concrete and meaningful situations. Hence spontaneous activities of the children should provide the natural condition for the growth of knowledge. This means that learning should be the result of doing. Nothing should be learned directly for its own sake.

Dewey believes that all true effort comes from a deep and natural interest in the task. If such an interest is absent, it is necessary to arouse it, because an artificial kindling of interest will be functionally bad. Dewey has declared that all learning which results from artificial stimulation is morally wrong. Therefore, learning, if it is to be moral and sound, must come forth as a result of the normal experience of the child. Thus, Dewey believes in the doctrine of natural interest, effort and motivation. It is from this doctrine that the Project Method has been evolved.

THE DISCIPLINE

Dewey is against the traditional conception of discipline. He does not believe in regulating the conduct of the pupil by artificial means. Dewey wants to emphasise the value of social life in his conception of discipline. By discipline in the school he means social discipline through and through. It is through this social discipline that he wants to develop the child as a member of the society. In this social discipline he gives full freedom to the natural impulses of the child. He wants to direct and discipline the natural inclinations of the child through the co-operative activities of the school. Through such a kind of training the child will develop a character which will be individually satisfying and socially useful.

Dewey believes that if the child's activities are purposeful and are carried out in co-operation with others, they will be disciplinary in their effect. If there are some common ends to be achieved, the relations between the various pupils in the school will be automatically characterized by discipline.

The teacher is not to impose himself on the pupils. He is not to be discipline-conscious. His sole function is to provide the right kind of environment so that the activities of the children may go on in a co-operative manner. The aim of discipline is to develop social studies, social interests, social habits, and social life.

Dewey does not realise the necessity of discipline in the school as a pre-condition for smooth work. But he holds that this discipline should not be aimed at as an end in itself. Respect for authority, patience and endurance have their place in life; but they should be the result of the child's appreciation of the value of leadership and necessity of rule and law in the school. No attempt should be made to develop them for their own sake. Thus, to Dewey, the purpose of discipline in the school is to produce a socialized individual who is conscious to develop himself fully and is always prepared to contribute his share to the social good.

Dewey has been greatly influenced both by Froebel and Herbart, but he differs from them basically. We shall compare below Dewey with Froebel and Herbart.

DEWEY AND FROEBEL

Dewey is not prepared to accept Froebel's conception of eternal or infinite growth, because this conception puts a limit to his notion of education as a continuous growth. Froebel's mysticism and symbolism do not harmonize with Dewey's pragmatism. Dewey has tried to re-interpret Froebel's concept of 'occupations'. He does not agree with the strange and occult meanings which Froebel attaches to them. He introduces new meanings to occupations by basing them on activities in relation to food, clothing and shelter. Dewey does not accept Froebel's stress on the spiritual. However, in certain respects Dewey and Froebel appear to be in general agreement; both emphasise creative activity, but in different ways; both believe in learning by doing; both accept the school as a living community in which children are engaged in co-operative social activities.

DEWEY AND HERBART

Dewey cannot agree with Herbart who stands for imparting knowledge to the child directly through teacher-control. However, Dewey will have no objection with Herbart when the latter emphasizes the need of arousing interest. Activity, problem, data, hypothesis and testing are the centre of Dewey's method of education; whereas Herbart stands for his formal steps — preparation, presentation, comparison, generalization and application. Thus to Dewey the child is the centre of the whole educational process, *i.e.*, it is the child who is to do everything; whereas to Herbart the teacher appears to occupy a prominent place, because it is the teacher who is already in the possession of the solution, and he has to pass it on to the passive child. Herbart stresses the activity of the teacher, and Dewey stresses the child as an active learner. Speaking on the Herbartian procedure and the Dewey's method Hornel says "The two methods admirably supplement each other; they are usable in different fields. Herbart is effective in the linguistic, literary, historical, and ideational fields; Dewey in the fields of the manual arts and sciences. Whenever the content of books is taught, Herbart is useful; wherever the manipulation of things is primary, Dewey is useful". It may be added here that Dewey's method is useful in the domain of ideas as well, and more so when "the approach to learning is through problem solving".

DEWEY : REALISM, IDEALISM AND NEO-SCHOLASTICISM

Dewey's doctrines are accepted by the pragmatists and experimentalists, but rejected by the idealists, the realists, and the neo-scholastics.

Realism

The realist is concerned with the world as it is. He wants to understand it. He does not mean to transform it as the pragmatist (or Dewey) wants to do. The realist wants to understand nature's laws so that he may adjusted to the existing scheme of things. To the realist there are existing indispensable facts and principles which must be mastered by the pupil; and it is the teacher's task to see that the pupil masters them perfectly with due effort. Evidently for this, the teacher must exercise some authority and he must keep the student under some discipline. Needless to say that the realist must be a bitter critic of Dewey's standpoints.

Idealism

To the pragmatist 'truth is relative'. To the idealist it is absolute. Dewey's philosophy emerges from naturalism and humanism, whereas idealism springs from theism. Dewey thinks that philosophy should concern itself with social conflicts arising from the interaction of industry, science, and democracy. He believes that intelligence which is to solve these social conflicts is just human to the idealist it is human as well as superhuman. To Dewey the basic principle of life and education is growth. The idealist accepts this point of view but goes further by stating that the growth must relate to more than the individual life. He wants to think of growth to the Infinite.

Dewey finds greater educational value in the activity produced by the impersonal relationship between the child and his problem situation. Thus to him, the teacher, though cannot be overlooked, is not so important as to the idealism who regards the teacher as the inspirer of the pupil.

Dewey emphasizes, interest, efforts and motivation. The idealist stresses effort, duty and discipline.

To Dewey education is a reconstruction of experience. To the idealist the function of education is to cultivate free personality. By education the idealist teacher wants to raise the pupil to the sublime realities and meaning of existence. To the idealist the man's potentialities kno no bounds. Hence his education will ever remai incomplete. However, education for the idealist does hav a definite goal.

Idealism appears to touch earth with heaven. considers man as the child of the Infinite. It believes i knowledge for the sake of knowledge, and also for th sake of life. It accepts an absolute goal for life an education. The position of idealism is unacceptable t Dewey, the pragmatist. To Dewey the term 'social' is mor meaningful than the intangible Infinite.

Neo-scholasticism

Besides realists and idealists, Robert Maynard Hutchins an ex-chancellor of the University of Chicago, an Mortimer J. Adler, professor of the philosophy of law a the University of Chicago, have been most vehement an bitter in criticising Dewey's educational philosophy an its influence in American education. These two critics an their followers are advocates of neo-scholasticism i American education. They want revive the medieva intellectualism in American education and denounce th vocationalism of higher education in America. Agains Dewey's philosophy Hutchins and his followers recommen the cultivation of the intellect. Against Dewey, the Hutchin school believes that the goals of education cannot b relative and variable. Hutchins urges that every on between the ages sixteen and twenty, except the obviousl unfit, must be given the same kind of general education Hutchins emphasizes the study of grammar, rhetoric, an logic and wants that every pupil should undergo thi disciplinary trio. The Hutchins school could get a natior wide publicity in America through many importan journals. But most of the schools of educational though in America have found fault in the Hutchins creed. Ever at the University of Chicago, where he has been at th helm for more than two decades since 1929, his majo philosophical principles have not been implemented 'hicago has not been able to do away with its utilitarian ɔurses. It still teaches courses in business, finance and anking.

DEWEY'S INFLUENCE

. has already been pointed out in the very beginning of ıis chapter that Dewey has exercised influence not only n American education but on education in foreign ɔuntries as well. Through his own efforts and through ıe efforts of his followers Dewey has contributed more ɔ the reconstruction and redirection of American ducation than any other single American. He accepted arker's theory of the school as a community and eveloped it much further. He developed the principle of rowth and showed new ways of realising the same. Dewey as been the first educator to found 'the school life and rogramme in the operational psychology of action'. Dewey ; a philosopher of revolt. He stood against the prevalent 'aditionalism in the school and tried to shape the school n a new line. He is the prophet of the experimental ıethod which has left a mark on education.

SUMMARY

ne of the greatest philosophers and educators of the 'orld. Enjoyed universal honour and fame.

ewey's Philosophy

Iind : Evolution of mind and intelligence in the natural ay. Result of man's activities to solve problems of life. Iind an effective instrument in solving problems. nowledge not apart from the mind. Instrumental theory : mind.

Knowledge : Knowledge result of action. Learning based ı experience. Knowledge not of independent existence — is always related to what man does or wants to do. ence knowledge should not be separated from action roducing it. Knowledge as a social instrument — a means for social progress. This standpoint one of his chie contributions.

The Process of Thinking : Thinking not in a vacuum does not originate from a mass of sensations. A problem stimulates thinking. Thinking a function of activity. Five logical steps in thinking.

Dewey's Philosophy of Education

What is Education : Education an indispensable socia process. Education a process of construction of experience Education begins since the very birth of the child and goes on throughout the whole life. Education a life itself.

The Aim of Education : No ultimate aim of education. Education has an immediate end. The aim of education in the process itself. No fixed goal to be achieved Education a continuous process of adjustment. The child to choose his own aim.

Education is Life Itself : No remote aim. The child live in the present. Future meaningless to him. The proces of education identical with the present life.

The Individual Factor in Education : The child the cor of the educational process. Child's interests and capacitie in a social context. Education to be based on the fou basic interests of the child — conversation, inquiry construction and artistic expression.

The Social Factor in Education : The individual nc apart from the society. The society an organic union c individuals. The family the first social institution. The chil to be helped to realise the purposes of society. Hence th school for co-operative action. This idea of socialization c highest importance.

The School

School essential to social life. At school the child to mak many experiments and learn. The school to produce social consciousness in the child. The school representative of the society outside. The school to gro out of the home life. The school to provide to the chi the home atmosphere in a more scientific form.

No formal moral lessons. Moral education through social activities. The school to make the society conscious of its needs and problems. The teacher a social servant.

The Curriculum

No sympathy with the traditional curriculum. No division of knowledge into particular branches. Activities of children should be the basis of school work.

Educative experiences and problems in the curriculum. The child to add to the existing ideas. Books, teachers and apparatus to be subordinated to the felt interest of the child.

The curriculum to develop critical discrimination in the pupil. The materials to be taught to be taken from the daily life. The present and the past to be linked together. Various subjects to be linked together.

The Method of Teaching

Direct experience as the basis. Spontaneous activities for the growth of knowledge. Learning by doing.

No artificial stimulation. Natural interest, effort and motivation. Project Method.

The Discipline

No artificial means for maintaining discipline. Social discipline in the school. Full freedom to the natural impulses of the child. Common ends will bring in discipline. The teacher not to impose himself. Social attitudes, interests, habits and will to be developed. The purpose of interest, discipline to produce a socialized individual.

Dewey and Froebel

Dewey against Froebel's conception of infinite growth, symbolism and mysticism. Dewey attaches new meanings to Froebel's 'occupations'. In certain respects the two are in general agreement. Both believe in creativity, learning by doing, and school as a community.

Dewey and Herbart

Herbart for teacher control. Dewey against it. Both for arousing interest. Herbart for his formal steps. Dewey for activity and problem, etc., etc. To Dewey the child is the centre. To Herbart the child is subordinated.

Dewey : Realism, Idealism and Neo-scholasticism

Realism : Realism does not want to transform the world as Dewey would like to do. The realist to make the child learn certain indispensable facts and principles. Dewey's standpoints not acceptable to the realist.

Idealism : To idealism truth is absolute — To Dewey— the pragmatist, it is relative. To the idealist intelligence is human and superhuman both. To Dewey the pragmatist, it is only human. To the idealist the teacher is the inspirer — To Dewey the problem situation is more important as an inspirer.

To Dewey education a reconstruction of experience — to the idealist it is a cultivation of free personality to sublime realities.

Neo-scholasticism : Hutchins and Adler its chief advocates in American education. Against the vocationalism of higher education in America. Against Dewey, they stand for the cultivation of intellect. Unlike Dewey, to them education cannot be relative and variable.

Dewey's Influence

Contributed more to the redirection and reconstruction of Education in America than any other single individual. Developed the theories of school as a community and growth, and showed ways of realising the same. A philosopher of revolt. Prophet of the experimental method.

References

1. Dewey, John : *How We Think*, pp. 11-12, D. C. Heath, Boston, 1910.
2. Dewey, John : *Democracy and Education*, p. 89, Macmillan, New York, 1916.
3. *Ibid*, p. 61.
4. Dewey, John : My Pedagogical Creeds Article I, The Progressive Education Association, Washington, D. C.
5. Dewey, John: *The School and Society* (Rev. Ed.) p. 45, University of Chicago Press, Chicago, 1915.
6. Dewey, John : My Pedagogical Creeds, Article III. The Progressive Education Association, Washington D.C.
7. Plan of Organization of the University Primary School, Privately printed.

13

SIR T. PERCY NUNN

(1870 — 1944)

His Life and Outlook

Sir T. Percy Nunn is one of the greatest educational philosophers that Great Britain has produced. He was appointed a professor of education in the University of London in 1917. He also held the post of Director of Institute of Education, London till 1936.

T. Percy Nunn has given importance to individualistic philosophy in education. In other words, he advocates free growth of personality. He has contended that whatever is attained in the world, comes from the right efforts of free personality. Therefore education should be organised for the development of free personality. He regards individual's powers higher than other powers in the world and he thinks that its fullest growth should be the chief aim of education. He has dealt with this individualistic philosophy in his famous book 'Education': Its 'Data and First Principles', published in 1920. Growth of personality takes place in society. So, social conditions affect personality. The responsibility of the growth to child's personality is on the teacher and his parents. So, the teacher and parents should provide the needed environment for the all sided growth of personality.

PSYCHOLOGICAL VIEW POINT OF NUNN

According to Nunn mind is not a group of free faculties. He divides activities of mind into two parts. His division is based on taking mind as one unit. He calls first part as Mneme, *i.e.*, power of acquisition and the second part as Horme, *i.e.* power of inspiration.

Mneme

Mind always collects experience. This is its natural trait. Nunn has called this simple power of collection as Mneme. Mneme is also active along with other activities. Memory is related to Mneme. The difference is that Mneme of mind is more powerful than the power of memory. Only special parts of collected ideas and influences come under the orbit of memory. Whereas power of collection *i.e.* Mneme puts activity into motion.

Forms of collected experiences change but the forms of their influences do not change. They remain in their own forms. These influences in the form of habits affect our ideas and experiences. Nunn has used the word 'Engram' for these influences.

Horme

Horme is that power of the mind which stimulates us into activity in order to reach a determined goal. One organises his duties, influences and activities according to this power as 'Horme' *i.e.*, 'power of purposiveness'. This power fills one with activity. Due to this power one advances towards his desired goal and tries to read it. This sort of inspiration is felt in the conscious part of the mind. Whereas, in digestion, resting, respiration and other functions, this power works on the unconscious level of the mind.

As far as education is concerned both the above mentioned aspects of mind's activities are important. With regard to the growth of children, educationists are divided into two schools of thought. Some educationists do not accept the contribution of environment in the growth of children. They regard heredity as thc original source of growth, whereas some others assign this importance to environment. Nunn follows the middle course. He thinks that the combination of heredity and environment gives rise to the process of growth. The child comes into this world inheriting traits of his ancestors and marches ahead into life employing environment usefully.

Environment helps in the modification and refinement of the traits inherited by the child. For full growth of the child both the inherited traits and environment should be taken into consideration.

NUNN'S VIEWS ON EDUCATION

Aims of Education

According to Nunn, the real aim of education is to create suitable environment for the highest development of personality. A child acquires different types of abilities at his different stages of growth. So studying the child's abilities and entrusting him the desired work according to his abilities, with a view to furthering the highest development of his personality should be the chief aim of education. Nunn thinks that pursuing suitable path each child can achieve success in developing his personality to the fullest extent according to his ability. Due to different kinds of abilities, different types of education for the development of individual abilities are required. So the same type of education can never be conducive to the right type of development of personality is the manifestation or the highest good of mankind. He is not in favour of collective education imparted from the socialistic standpoint. But being against socialistic standpoint and emphatic on individualistic system of education, he does not want that one should neglect his duty towards society. He believes that the growth of the individual is possible only in society. But at the same time he does not want to neglect the individual. He advocates the growth and progress of society by developing the individual personality of each child. Thus he regards society as helpful for the development of personality. So he is not an extreme individualist. He stands for a harmony between the individual and social aim of education. The first is the personality development view and the second is the welfare of society as a whole.

Curriculum

According to Nunn, school is not only a place of earning knowledge but a place of bringing excellence in the activites of children as well. In order to make children conversant with thoughts concerning individual and society suitable subjects should be included in the curriculum. Environment and living-begins to leave a deep impression on the child. According to Nunn, science is of great importance in the curriculum. He believes that schools are parts of the nation. The main task of schools is to provide spiritual strength to the nation, to maintain historical links and to preserve antiquities. They have to ensure success in future. Therefore, Nunn has attached great importance to the study of humanities as well. Thus Nunn's viewpoint regarding curriculum is, in a way, similar to that of idealists. Nunn idealises his individualistic philosophy. He gives importance to such subjects in the curriculum which may be helpful in creating civilization. He lays importance on bringing up society to the highest peak of civilization through constructive activities. He has given place to geography and history in the curriculum along with literature, music, art, craft and science.

Importance of Play in Education

There is a craving for self-expression in the heart of every one. The child expresses this urge in his plays. With this view Nunn accepts play as an important tool of education. Play is a noble manifestation of the constructive tendency of self expression. Child's interests may be estimated through his plays. Body gets strong by play. Play is helpful in developing morality and practicability. It is an instrument of inspiring children for the solution of some knotty problems of life.

Play and Work

According to Nunn a child takes a work as a play, which he does out of his own will, and when he is forced to do something he takes it as a work. Certain things we feel compelled to do, *e.g.*, we eat to live. Certain work we do out of our own will. We do not need any pressure from outside for doing it, *e.g.*, playing football. Play gives peace to many natural faculties of the child. In play there is freedom along with perseverance. Play may be divided into many parts :

(1) For utilising leisure,
(2) Constructive,
(3) Emulating,
(4) Educative,
(5) Serious and higher types of play.

If we divide play into groups, we shall get the same groups of work. Highest work and highest play are equal in all respects. There remains no difference in their essential spirit.

Place of Freedom in Education

Man is born free in the world. So he requires freedom for his proper development in every sphere of life. Nunn does not see play and freedom in different aspects. He accepts both almost in the same connotation. Nunn gives importance to freedom in education, but he does not want to bring indiscipline by giving undue liberty. He regards unrestrained natural development of the child as the aim of educational freedom and for the process of this development he accepts the restraint of the desired rules. Making the child free from the burden of checks, he thinks it more proper to develop him by observing helpful theoretical principles.

Freedom and Discipline

Evidently, where Nunn emphasises the natural development of the child, the also wants to restrain that development. Unless the mind of the child develops a little, Nunn gives responsibility of discipline to the teacher. But he does not grant freedom to the teacher in putting unnecessary hurdles in the work of children. In his opinion, a teacher should only interfere in a child's work, when his actions are so directed as to obstruct the growth of others. He regards work as a companion of discipline. He wants that the responsibility of discipline should be given to the disciplined children and partly to the teachers instead of giving it to others. But a teacher should be very careful in exercising discipline and restraint. Nunn has not taken discipline and school order as synonyms. If he regards discipline as soul, he regards school order as body. School order is an outer manifestation of class peace, while discipline implies inner tendencies. A suitable environment is needed in education in order to give freedom a nobler form so that the child, after developing understanding, may be able to observe proper rules and principles himself. In this way, principles of discipline will themselves promote freedom.

Organisation of Education

Systematic development of the child's mind is the purpose of education. In order to make this task easy and useful, schools have been divided scientifically into groups. Ordinarily, the school has been organised into two types, primary and secondary. But Nunn wants to organise education into three parts on the basis of children's feelings and development. These parts are the mile-stones of physical and mental development of children. They are: (1) Infancy, (2) Childhood, and (3) Adolescence. Infancy lasts upto the age of 6 or 8 years. A child at this stage should be educated in infant schools under Froebel and Montessori systems. Childhood lasts nearly upto 13 years of age. During this period education may be imparted in primary schools. The third stage of education for adolescent period is a very important period in life according to Nunn. Children receive education in secondary schools during this period. This is a period of secondary education. This educational period lasts upto 18 years of age or so. Towards close of this period boys and girls grow the feeling of manhood and womanhood. Nunn has regarded it as an aid to receive higher education. He recognizes the importance of secondary education in its own right.

SUMMARY

Individualistic Philosophy

Nunn believes in the free development of human tendencies. He is opposed to the social bonds that obstruct the free growth of personality. He believes in the supreme force of personality. The personality is formed by the views and concepts that a man holds about life and various other things. Individualism of Nunn aims at providing an atmosphere conducive to growth of personality. It does not come in clash with society, but on the contrary, seeks it assistance in its development.

The Psychological Standpoint

Nunn does not accept mind as an independent force. According to him, it has two distinct activities — Mneme and Horme. Former preserves the experiences and the latter is the basic stimulating force. In the field of education these two forces play a vital role.

Views on Education

Nunn holds that the real purpose of education is to provide the necessary environment for the attainment of perfection and development of personality.

Curriculum : About curriculum, Nunn's views are akin to those of idealists. He lays emphasis on assigning an important place in curriculum to literature, music, art, handicraft, science, geography, history and other such subjects which help in preservation of past achievements and furtherance of civilization.

Play : Through plays the inner-most and constructive desire of self-manifestation is achieved. When one performs an act voluntarily, he does that in playful spirit. Nunn has given an important place to play in education. Plays are helpful in developing the morals and interests of children.

Freedom : Nunn believes in freedom in education. But to avoid freedom from being misguided, he wants some control, also to be exercised. He makes no discinction between freedom and play.

Organisation of Education : Nunn has divided education in three stages : (1) Infant education, which is to be provided in nursery schools. (2) Child education — Arrangement for this should be made in primary schools. (3) Education of Adolescents (Between the age of 12 and 18). Education at this stage should be given in secondary schools.

14

BERTRAND RUSSELL

(1872 — 1971)

His Life

Bertrand Russell was born on May 18, 1872 at Trelleck, Wales. His parents died when he was only three years old. He was, therefore, brought up by his grand-parents. He learnt German and French from a tutor and made a mark in both the languages. He was admitted to the Trinity College, Cambridge, in 1890. He distinguished himself as a brilliant student, securing first class and distinction in philosophy. He also won the highest honour of Wrangler. In recognition of this honour he was made a fellow of the college in 1895, but could not accept this honour as while in the college in 1893, he had already accepted an offer for a job under the British Embassy in France. He left the college to join it. He was attracted by Peano's works on mathematics. He read them thoroughly. His first book 'Principles of Mathematics' was published in 1903. In the year 1910 he was appointed as a lecturer in his old college. When the First World War broke out in 1914 he took active part in the "No Conscription Fellowship" and was fined £100. His personal library was confiscated for the realisation of the fine and he was removed also from the service of the college. He got another appointment as a teacher in Harvard but was refused the passport to go there.

He was awarded six months' imprisonment for his article published in the Tribunal. "Introduction of

Mathematical Philosophy" his world famous book was written in jail. He was invited by Peking University in 1920 for giving lectures on philosophy. Below we give a list of some of his more outstanding works :

(1) The A.B.C. of Atoms (1923),
(2) The A.B.C. of Relativity (1925),
(3) On Education (1926),
(4) The Analysis of Matter
(5) Principia Mathematics (1925)
(6) The Outline of Philosophy (1928)
(7) Marriage and Morals (1929).
(8) The Conquest of Happiness (1930).
(9) The Scientific Outlook (1931).
(10) Education and the Social Order (1932).
(11) Freedom and Organisation, 1814—1914 (1934).
(12) Power : A New Social Analysis (1938).
(13) An Enquiry into Meaning and Truth (1940).
(14) Sceptical Essays (1920).
(15) Power : A New Social Analysis (1938).
(16) A History of Western Philosophy (1946).
(17) Human Knowledge, Its Scope and Limits (1948).
(18) Authority and The Individual (1949).
(19) New Hopes for a Changing World (1951).
(20) The Impact of Science on Society (1952).

He was awarded the Noble Prize in literature in 1950.

Logic is the corner stone of Russell's philosophy. He has revised his views on ethics, metaphysics, Nature, etc. in the light of his personal experiences from time to time. He does not like his philosophy to be placed in the category of idealism or realism. He likes it to be classed in logical atomism. He thinks that one can realise the basic reality of a thing through logical analysis. He gives place both to philosophy and mathematics in his philosophical thinking. He is an outstanding philosopher and reformer and emphasises the importance of creative attitude. He is profoundly interested in the basic problems of human beings. In fact, he has sacrificed his entire life for the welfare of mankind. His vehement protest against nuclear weapons and wars in the world is an eloquent testimony to this. He has subjected himself to many hardships and sufferings on account of his unflinching adherence to his views. He may rightly be described as a *Rishi* (Seer) of the modern age.

Volumes may be written on the different aspects of Bertrand Russell's ideas. But within the very limited scope of this small chapter we shall discuss here only some of his main views on education.

PURPOSE OF EDUCATION

According to Russell the teacher should strive for inculcating four principal qualities in children. The inculcation of these qualities is the main purpose of education. These qualities are : (1) Vitality, (2) Courage, (3) Sensitiveness, and (4) Intelligence. We shall discuss each of these below :

(1) *Vitality*

Vitality is found in persons who are physically fit in all respects. The age, too, has a direct bearing on vitality. Vitality diminishes as one advances in age and at the old age it is at its lowest. Vitality is a human characteristic related more to physical than mental conditions. It reaches fullness in the very early years of a healthy child. The effect of vitality is that it intensifies pleasure in life. It is the face which motivates an individual to do various kind of things.

(2) *Courage*

It is not easy to define courage. It has many forms. The person possessing courage is capable of keeping fears both rational and irrational under control. The behaviour of person in grave hours affords an opportunity to others to judge his courage. The person who does not lose self-control even when confronted with natural calamities such as earthquake, fire, and storms or lays down his life willingly in the battle field rather than turning the back may be regarded a person of courage. Courage is a precious virtue of human beings. So every man and woman should try to develop it. Undue display of courage is, however, to be avoided as a socially undesirable behaviour. It should find expressions in our thought, word and deed. Every child should be trained to develop the virtue of courage. This should be one of the chief purposes of education.

(3) *Sensitiveness*

Sensitiveness is related to our emotions. A large number of children cross the limit of sensational pleasure at the age of 5 years and develop desire for socially approved pleasures. When this sort of pleasure starts growing in the child the speed of his development is accelerated. Every child during this period hates, blames and loves praises. The desire to get social pleasures generally persists life-long in an individual. It, therefore, may act as a powerful stimulus to make the child do noble deeds. Emergence of sympathy is also a form of sensitiveness. A small child starts weeping when he sees his own brother or sister weeping. This is an example of physical sympathy. The physical sympathy is the foundation for further growth of sympathy in a child. The development of sympathy in a child should be so controlled through education that he may have sympathy for his friends or relations even when they are not present in person. Sympathy should be developed to such a degree that it may find expression not only when a person has actually been taken over by adversity but even at the very apprehension of the befalling calamity. A sympathy of this sort widens the outlook. Russell is of the view that the cognitive and aesthetic sensitiveness should similarly be developed in the child, as one of primary purposes of education.

(4) *Intelligence*

It should also be one of the main purposes of education to develop intelligence in children. The mental life of a child is manifested in the curiosity he expresses for various things in his surroundings. Russell says that education should aim at giving a desired direction to the child's curiosity. Curiosity may be useful to a person only when it is related to some means for acquiring knowledge. Power of observation, patience, industriousness and faith are some of the qualities which spring forth spontaneously in a person possessing curiosity.

Russell thinks that happiness in human life is possible only if the four qualities of vitality, courage, sensitiveness and intelligence are developed through education. In this way a new world may be created for man. But it will be too much to say that these four qualities complete the list and leave no room for additions. Russell believes firmly that these qualities spring up without much difficultly in a child, if adequate arrangements are made for his physical, emotional and intellectual development.

GENERAL PRINCIPLES OF EDUCATION

The first six years of a child's life are very important. Russell thinks that a child of six years of age needs intellectual training. Moral teaching is not useful to a young child, as it does not good either to his intellectual or character development before he develops the power of judgment. From the child's point of view things taught to him should have two main purposes : Firstly, the development of curiosity which constitutes the basis of intellectual development; secondly, the child should be taught skills which he may use for satisfying his curiosities through his own efforts. The teacher should also be careful to provide stimuli to awaken curiosity in children. In no case the curiosity of a child should be suppressed. It is quite likely that sometimes the curiosity expressed by the child may be of such a nature that it may be difficult to satisfy it through the teaching in the school. In such a situation the teacher should advise the child about the other means through which he should try to satisfy his curiosity at other hours.

It is necessary for a child to grow some special qualities in him in order to acquire various types of knowledge. These special qualities may be mentioned as intellectual virtues. More important among these virtues are the following :

(1) Curiosity, (2) Open-mindedness, (3) Faith in acquiring knowledge, (4) Perseverance, (5) Concentration, (6) Patience, and (7) Exactness. We shall explain these qualities below one by one and give the views of Russell on each.

(1) *Curiosity* : According to Russell the trait of curiosity is very necessary for acquiring of knowledge. In fact, it forms the very basis of knowledge. If a child is in possession of keen curiosity and it has been given a turn to the right direction, other virtues as mentioned above will follow automatically.

(2) *Open-mindedness* : Open-mindedness is also necessary for acquiring knowledge. This trait exists in all those persons who have real thirst for knowledge.

(3) *Faith in Acquisition of Knowledge* : Faith in acquisition of knowledge is the first step towards acquiring knowledge. A feeling of this kind helps one to become active. Russell urges that this faith must be created in the child.

(4) *Perseverance* : Though perseverance one can do any thing. Russell underlines the need for inculcating and strengthening the spirit of perseverance in children through education. The ambition for victory over difficulty should be aroused for this purpose among children.

(5) *Concentration* : Russell attaches particular significance to concentration. He says that concentration is the most precious virtue in human being and it may be created only through education. As a matter of fact, this virtue develops to a certain extent in a natural way also. A young child can concentrate on an object only for a few seconds. He will talk about something at one moment and quite another at the next. This is the case with his thinking process also. The child should be trained to develop his power of concentration. The teacher should be specially conscious for the development of this trait in the child.

(6) *Patience* : There is no doubt about the possibility

of acquiring knowledge, but it needs patience and hard labour. Russell is therefore, of the opinion that students should be trained to develop patience in them.

(7) *Exactness* : Russell accepts the importance of exactness in the process of learning. How far person is devoted to truth may be guessed through the degree of exactness which he manifests in his behaviour. Hence the quality of exactness should be developed in child.

NURSERY SCHOOL

Who should be entrusted with the responsibility of inculcating desirable habits in the young child within 3 or 4 years of age ? Should the task be entrusted to parents or to schools organised specially for this purpose ? Russell says that this work should be given to nursery schools. In the present day-conditions, it is not possible for parents to discharge this responsibility satisfactorily. The nursery schools, therefore, should be organised on a large scale to make the necessary facilities available to each young child. The children admitted to these schools should learn something more beyond reading and writing. Not only the accuracy in their sense-perception, but their acquaintance with basic principles of music, dance, drawing is also necessary at this stage.

CURRICULUM FOR CHILDREN WITHIN 5 AND 14 YEARS OF AGE

The subjects that require greater mental exercise may be begun by and by during childhood, *i.e.* within 5 and 14 years of age. For example, we may start teaching mathematics to a child after he completes seven years of age.

Russell says that efforts should be made to acquaint children with the general geographical and historical topics. These topics should be presented before children in an interesting manner. In teaching geography pictures should be used and adventurous tales should be narrated to make the subject more interesting. Children have a natural liking for stories and pictures. They should know at this stage that there are countries of different climates and people of different types in the world. Russell believes that this kind of knowledge will help the development of imaginative power in children. The geography books approved for children should contain pictures and maps in sufficient number, besides the general information about the different parts of the world.

History should not be taught to children upto the first 5 years of age. The use of pictures and stories should be made in teaching history. Stories of great men of the world should also be taught to them. Teachers while teaching history should note the interests of children. Russell suggests that while giving children an account of man at the primitive stage suitable pictures should be utilized in order to explain clearly the insecurity that man had to face in his early stage and the hazards of nature to which he was exposed then. The picture should depict how man lived solely on fruits and raw vegetables. It should also be explained through pictures to them how fire was discovered and how it influenced the human life. The entire process of evolution of social and economic life of man should be explained to them stage by stage. A clear idea should be given to them that man at first began his life by roaming about from one place to another in search of fruits and water. Then he domesticated animals at a later stage. This, however, did not bring end of his wandering life. He had to move with his cattle in search of new meadows. This brought him at places where some kind of wild paddy grew. This gave him an idea of sowing seeds and producing greater quantity of grains at one place. Ultimately he took to agriculture and started it in valleys. The children should also be told how the social life of man started taking shape after his inhabitation on land for agricultural purposes. Gradual formation of family, village, cities and country should be explained to them. The child should be told how man learnt reading, writing and science or other things. We are not to remain silent about wars and other upheavals. We are however, to be careful that in giving the accounts of wars we do not involved in depicting glories of military conquests. The emphasis should be on describing the greatness of such personalities as Buddha, Socrates, Newton, Gandhi and others.

Russell is in favour of affording opportunities to children for learning music, dance and acting because these improve the health of children and develop their aesthetic sense.

About language, Russell is not in favour of teaching too many of them. In this regard the aptitude of children should be taken into consideration. They may be taught one or two foreign languages in addition to their mother tongue. In choice of foreign languages an international point of view should be the major consideration. As regards literature, only certain pieces should be selected for them. In making the selection, the major interests of children should be the guiding factor.

The teaching of algebra, physics and chemistry should not be begun before the age of 12 years. Some classical language may also be taught to children within the age group of 12 and 15, if they show any interest for them. No specialization is to be attempted at this level.

EDUCATION FOR CHILDREN BETWEEN 14-18

According to Russell specialization in a particular area may be allowed during the 14 - 18 age group. But only the children with above average intelligence should be encouraged for specialization.

The subjects in which opportunities should be available for specialization in the school according to Russell fall into three categories : (1) Classics, (2) Mathematics and Science, and (3) Modern humanities. Some special knowledge in respect of each of these categories may be acquired before a student leaves the school. The studies in mathematics, science and classics should continue simultaneously. Facilities for specialization should be given to students according to their abilities and aptitudes. Modern humanities include modern languages, literature and history. In these as well, each student should be given special education according to his particular aptitude.

Every student should be taught rudiments of anatomy, physiology and hygiene, because one must know something of each of these sciences in order to understand the basic principles of health and hygienic living. The teacher should teach these subjects in such a manner that the students do not feel bored. For this, he should have perfect mastery over the subject-matter and should be able to connect it with various life-situations in a relevant manner.

The students in the class have not to be passive listeners. In fact, they should be active partners in the efforts of the teacher. In the traditional school more emphasis was laid on class work than on individual work. Russell is against the practices of the traditional school. He recommends that the school should encourage co-operative endeavour in the class, as this will develop both the individual and social personality of the student.

The school is a society in miniature, the purpose of which is to prepare students for adjustments in future life in a bigger society. So it is necessary that students should learn also about the current social, political and theological problems.

We are to produce men and women of independent thinking in our schools. It is necessary for this purpose that we give ample time to students for free exchange of thought. We should not prove a hinderance in the way of their independent thinking and free criticism. We are not to sacrifice their individuality at the alter of so-called accepted moral values. Russell is of the view that every individual should be tested on the touch-stone of intellect in the pursuit of truth. We are to develop and train the various impulses of students in such a way tat that they acquire virtues themselves. What Russell really means is the development of a scientific spirit in students.

UNIVERSITY EDUCATION

Russell thinks that university education should be imparted only to a selected few. All the students at the higher secondary school level are not fit for university education. Therefore, only suitable students should be sent for higher education in universities.

The problem arises about the selection of students for university education. Now-a-days students going for university education are mostly from rich families. But in the matter of selection of the right type of students for university eduction emphasis will have to be shifted from economic soundness to the ability of students. Before we decide anything final about selection of students, it is necessary to give some thought to the purpose of university education.

According to Russell university education has two purposes. The first is to prepare persons for certain professions and the second relates to learning and research. So only those students should be allowed admission to universities who are either to be prepared for certain professions or have an ability and aptitude for research in some area.

Russell thinks that university education instead of being prerogative of a few rich people should be a privilege of all. No such student should be allowed admission to a university who fails to get through the examination prescribed for this purpose. Even when the admission has once been obtained, it should be made necessary for the students to satisfy the teachers concerned through their work failing which they should be removed. In fact, universities are to be made temples of learning where intelligent and diligent persons find place and not clubs for easy going persons. This may be possible only when both the people and the government get ready for the necessary sacrifice for making arrangements to ensure freedom from financial worries to every teacher and student in the university. What should be the measuring rod of the diligent and intelligent students? The current type of examination is not suitable to assess the ability of a student. Methods of working in universities will have to be modified. How can this be done? Russell thinks that at the beginning of an academic session the students should be advised to study some such books which might be considered necessary for all and they should also be advised to read some books according to their curiosity which is sure to differ from person to person. The teacher is to play his role both in individual and collective capacity. He, while guiding the students collectively by giving advice and information on the latest researches on various subjects, should also strive to remove the individual difficulties of students. The papers set for assessing the ability of the students should also be so prepared that only those students may give satisfactory answer who have carefully studied the prescribed books.

Russell believes that the teacher who does not keep the flame of knowledge burning is incapable of throwing light of knowledge on the path of those who come to universities in search of it. This view emphasises the need of entrusting the university education to such teachers who are intellectual giants in their chosen spheres of knowledge and are prepared to put in their heart and soul together in doing further researches in the subjects of their interest. This standard may be attained by a university teacher when he is free from the daily worries of life and gets ample time to devote to the pursuit of knowledge and has also been accorded a place of respect in society.

Russell advises that the university teacher after every seven years should be given one year's time to devote exclusively to studying the work carried on in various countries in his subject.

SUMMARY

The Purpose of Education : The aim of education is to develop the following four virtues in every individual:

(1) Vitality,
(2) Courage,
(3) Sensitiveness, and
(4) Intelligence.

General Principle of Education : Education prescribed for a child after the age of six, should be free from moral ideals and provide largely for purely intellectual training.

It should also be aimed simultaneously that the child becomes capable of satisfying his curiosities through his own efforts. His curiosities should not be suppressed. The children should be encouraged to develop the following mental qualities :

(1) Curiosity,
(2) Open-mindedness,
(3) Faith,
(4) Perseverance,
(5) Concentration,
(6) Patience, and
(7) Exactness.

Nursery School : Inculcation of desirable habits in children should be the primary function of nursery schools. Parents cannot develop these qualities in children. Hence the necessity of nursery schools.

Curriculum for Children Within 5 and 14 : The life of a person may be divided into four parts, *i.e.*, childhood, adolescence, youth and old age. Each of these has its own needs and characteristics which should be kept in view in the process of education. Literature, mathematics, science, geometry, algebra, physics, chemistry should be taught when a child has attained the age of twelve. Efforts should also be made to ascertain a child's special interests.

Education for Children Between 14 and 18 : Arrangements for special education should be made only for those students who are above average in intelligence.

The subjects which may be taken up for special studies in the school may be the following :

(1) Classics
(2) Mathematics and Science
(3) Modern humanities or other modern subjects. Instruction in physiology and hygiene should be made available, to a certain degree, to all boys and girls.

No student should be a passive listener. He should be

an active participant in the co-operative educational activities. The main task of a teacher is to supervise the activities of the students and help and guide them when and where necessary. Students should also be given opportunities for working independently.

University Education : University education should be only for the selected few intelligent and diligent students.

The purpose of university education are two—first, to prepare and train persons for certain professions, and secondly to provide for learning and research.

These objectives of university education may be achieved when intelligence and diligent students alone are admitted.

Correct assessment of ability of student is not possible unless present method of university education is suitably modified.

The university teacher should be an intellectual giant with profound interest in teaching work.

INDEX